AMERICAN VOICES

AMERICAN VOICES

An Integrated Skills Reader

Ruth M. Jackson
Robert J. Di Pietro

University of Delaware
Newark, Delaware

Heinle & Heinle Publishers
A Division of Wadsworth, Inc.
Boston, Massachusetts 02116

Photo Credits

opposite 1   George Holton, Photo Researchers, Inc.; **15**   Owen Franken, Stock, Boston; **20**   Rafael Macia, Photo Researchers, Inc.; **30**   Charles Kennard, Stock, Boston; **34**   Jim Whitmer, Stock, Boston; **48**   Spencer Grant, Stock, Boston; **52**   The Bettmann Archive; **61**   Andy Levin, Photo Researchers, Inc.; **64**   Michael Weisbrot, Stock, Boston; **77**   Bob Daemmrich, The Image Works, Inc.; **82**   Courtney Clarke, Photo Researchers, Inc.; **94**   Marcello Bertinetti, Photo Researchers, Inc.; **98**   Jean-Claude Lejeune, Stock, Boston; **109**   The Bettmann Archive; **112**   UPI/Bettmann Newsphotos; **120**   Jacques Chenet, Woodfin Camp & Associates, Inc.; **124**   The Bettmann Archive; **136**   UPI/Bettmann; **140**   Inge Morath, Magnum Photos; **148**   Franco Zecchin, Magnum Photos

Text Design: Carla Bolte
Cover Design: Viqui Maggio
Project Management: Hockett Editorial Service

American Voices An Integrated Skills Reader

Manufactured in the United States of America

Library of Congress Cataloging-in-Publication Data

Jackson, Ruth M.
    American voices : an integrated skills reader / Ruth M. Jackson and Robert J. Di Pietro.
        p.   cm.
    ISBN: 0-8384-3847-4
    1. English language—Textbooks for foreign speakers.   2. Readers—United States.   3. United States—Civilization—Problems, exercises, etc.   I. Di Pietro, Robert J.   II. Title.
    PE1128.J25   1992b
    428.6'4—dc20   91-28550
                                                                      CIP

10   9   8   7   6   5   4   3   2   1

Dedication
To my beautiful mother, who taught
"All are precious in His sight . . . ."
RMJ

In memory of Sebastiano Giallo and Maria Bongiorno Giallo,
whose presence is felt in these pages.
RDP

Contents

Preface

American Voices is an interactive, integrated-skills reader for advanced and high-advanced ESL/EFL students. It is also a reader for university-level cultural-diversity classes and for classes in advanced composition for native writers. This book can be used in any learning situation in which the teachers' aims are to promote cross-cultural understanding and to develop students' skills in thinking and communicating to their full potential.

The book's ten chapters offer a range of content-based materials about the cultural composition of the United States. Its contents are designed to stimulate students' thinking and to inspire them to find their own voices—to help them move from Stage 4 of the reading and writing processes to Stage 5, where they are *independent* thinkers and *creators* of new ideas and schemata. The activities and exercises give students the opportunity to clarify their thinking and to examine their values while they are integrating their listening and speaking skills with their reading and writing skills. In each chapter, students listen to, discuss, read about, and write about experiences which people face in ordinary life. In these interactions, and in the learner-centered environment which this text induces, students can acquire the target language naturally and optimally.

Each chapter consists of eight parts. The first part is a scenario, which provides a concrete experience with natural language, establishes (and subsequently reinforces) the interactive nature of the classroom, and sets up a situation or problem which the class must work on together to resolve. The scenario is the keystone for all subsequent schema building that will go on in the chapter. Discussion, in the form of debriefing questions, follows the scenario and allows students to clarify their own beliefs, the beliefs of others, and points of grammar, syntax, semantics, and pragmatics. The third part, suggestions for further activities, allows students to do further schema building as necessary, or as the teacher may choose to do.

Next, students read an excerpt from an ethnic American writer. The purpose of using ethnic literature is two-fold. First, for ESL/EFL students, such content can enable them to see something of themselves in the experiences of these authors and, by realizing that they are not alone in their struggles to survive in a land where they are culturally and linguistically special, to take some comfort in this fact. For students enrolled in cultural-diversity classes, these reading passages can help them appreciate the richness and the variety of American voices. Second, a passage from ethnic literature can allow all students to "hear" voices from the home and hearth—in both a literal *and* a metaphoric sense. In the dialogues, for example, students can study the stress, tone, and pitch which speakers of languages other than English use as they become familiar with English. ESL/EFL students can then look at their *own* stage in language development and become more aware of the differences between their native languages and English. After the reading, students are asked to prepare answers to discussion questions. This work can be done in pairs or in small groups. These questions require critical thinking and values clarification.

The sixth activity is interactive grammar and usage. Working with a partner, the student is asked to choose answers to complete a passage coherently and cohesively. Then, in class discussion, students must provide the reason for their choices. This exercise develops cognitive skills, as students are led to an awareness of the structures, semantics, and pragmatics involved in the process of selecting the best answers. After completing the passage, they can be asked to induce and state the rules on which they have based their choices. Thus, they are learning grammar in a natural and communicative way, rather than by rote memorization.

The seventh activity increases students' word power. By working with a partner and making judicious guesses about the meanings of words in context, each student builds meaning in a way that is common in natural discourse. To add further lexical dimensions of meaning, students are then encouraged to look up the words in a monolingual dictionary.

The final part of each unit is designed to help students find their own voices in the target language. Assignments for discussion and writing are included in this part to provide students with the opportunity to determine what they think and feel about the subjects and experiences they have been studying and with the opportunity to express those thoughts and emotions in a focused, effective manner.

The most significant approaches used in this text are the Experiential Learning Cycle (adapted from Kolb's book *Experiential Learning*); the principles of values clarification (as established by Raths et al. in *Values and Teaching*, and as employed so effectively by Freire in his literacy circles—see *Pedagogy of the Oppressed*); and in the use of the scenario (as developed by Di Pietro in *Strategic Interaction*). *American Voices* is grounded in learner-centered education, the principles of which we are deeply committed to cultivating.

A few final comments about the reading excerpts: the subject matter of the excerpts is, for the most part, serious. We were deliberate in choosing them, for understanding across cultures *is* a serious matter, requiring ongoing adjustments and tolerance as peoples from other countries become our neighbors and work together with us to create new and better lives. Each of the readings included here provides an intimate look into the kinds of problems and concerns which ordinary people often have. Each of us, whether we are new to a culture or "old" members of it, faces problems; but these problems can become even larger when the language needed to survive is not our native tongue or is not readily at our command. Real people are portrayed here, dealing with very real experiences as they make adjustments to life in their new homes in America.

ESL/EFL students will, we hope, be able to see something of themselves in the experiences of the authors represented here and thereby realize that they are not alone in struggling with the novelty of a new life in an alien land. For Americans already familiar with English, our hope is that the rich diversity of cultures portrayed in this book will heighten their awareness of the beauty and vigor with which Americans express themselves. But most important, this book has been designed to encourage its readers to add their *own* voices to those represented here.

◆ Acknowledgments

We wish to thank our students, from whom we continually learn; the director of the University of Delaware's English Language Institute, Dr. Scott G. Stevens, for his encouragement and support; associate director Kathy Schneider, for wishing us luck; and our colleague and friend, Sandra McCollum, who always gave willingly of her critical acumen and her empathy. Also from Ruth, the deepest appreciation to dear, dear friends, Nan, Bill, and Ian Marcus, whose love, laughter, and abiding faith inspire.

Ruth M. Jackson
Robert J. Di Pietro

AMERICAN VOICES

CHAPTER 1

African American

◆ Listening to Each Other: Scenario

A scenario is an activity which will provide you with the opportunity to interact with fellow students and to do some negotiating of your own choosing. Playing in scenarios will help you to acquire vocabulary and to prepare for discussion, debate, reading, and writing.

Your teacher will assign roles to you to enact in the scenario. First, separate groups of students will each get a role. Then, each group will have some time to work on the task associated with the role. When you are sufficiently prepared, one member of your group will play the role in interaction with someone from the other group or groups. During this performance of the roles, you may stop the conversation in order to return to your group for advice and help. Afterward, the teacher will lead the entire class in a discussion of the performance, touching on important words, grammatical constructions, and other matters pertinent to the interaction.

You should take notes during all phases of the scenario (preparation, performance, and discussion), as you see fit. These notes will help you in future conversations and interactions.

Prepare and perform the scenario "The search for one's roots."

◆ Speaking Out: Debriefing Questions

1. Identify and discuss any differences in attitudes among the scenario participants about working and visiting relatives in the country of an-

cestors referred to in the scenario. Are any of these differences *generational*?

2. If you are or if you plan to become a citizen of the United States, have you maintained contact with your homeland and relatives? How important is doing so to you and to your family?

3. If you are visiting or studying in the United States and plan to return home in the near future, how important to you is it to stay in touch with people in your home country?

4. Do you identify with any character in the scenario? If so, which one? Explain why you empathized with that person.

5. Would you change anything if the scenario were acted out again?

◆ Reaching Out: Suggestions for Further Activities

1. Go to the library and locate some books which tell the life stories of African slaves in the United States (for example, Harriet Tubman). Prepare a presentation in which you become that person and tell "your" life story to your classmates.

2. Research the history of the movement known as the "Harlem Renaissance." Who were the important figures in this movement? Whom did they influence? If possible, visit a nearby library and consult its offerings in black studies. The Langston Hughes Library at Lincoln University, Lincoln, Pennsylvania, for example, contains an extensive collection of books and manuscripts by black American authors and on black American history.

3. African Americans have made many outstanding contributions to the development of culture and of the sciences in the United States. Choose one such black woman or man and give a short presentation to your class about that person.

4. If possible, watch the first part of the television miniseries "Roots." Take notes on Kunta Kinte's story. Then read the selection from the book *Roots*. How closely does the miniseries presentation follow Haley's book?

5. Write an essay about one aspect of the scenario and bring it into class for the group to critique and polish.

◆ Reading: From *Roots*, by Alex Haley

Read the following selection, keeping in mind the scenario you have already experienced. It is always a good idea to have an English-English dictionary at hand when you read. A useful technique is to read the selection through quickly the first time, highlighting words or phrases that you think you need to look up. Then go back and do a more careful reading, looking up unfamiliar words.

CHAPTER 120

1 Soon after, I went to the National Archives in Washington, D.C., and told a reading-room desk attendant that I was interested in Alamance County, North Carolina, census records just after the Civil War. Rolls of microfilm were delivered. I began turning film through the machine, feeling a mounting sense of intrigue while viewing an endless parade of names recorded in that old-fashioned penmanship of different 1800s census takers. After several of the long microfilm rolls, tiring, suddenly in utter astonishment I found myself looking down there on: "Tom Murray, black, blacksmith—," "Irene Murray, black, housewife—" . . . followed by the names of Grandma's older sisters—most of whom I'd listened to countless times on Grandma's front porch. "Elizabeth, age 6"—nobody in the world but my Great Aunt Liz! At the time of that census, Grandma wasn't even born yet!

2 It wasn't that I hadn't believed the stories of Grandma and the rest of them. You just *didn't* not believe my grandma. It was simply so uncanny sitting staring at those names actually right there in official U.S. Government records.

3 Then living in New York, I returned to Washington as often as I could manage it—searching in the National Archives, in the Library of Congress, in the Daughters of the American Revolution Library. Wherever I was, whenever black library attendants perceived the nature of my search, documents I'd requested would reach me with a miraculous speed. From one or another source during 1966, I was able to document at least the highlights of the cherished family story; I would have given anything to be able to tell Grandma—then I would remember what Cousin Georgia had said, that she, all of them, were "up there watchin'."

4 Now the thing was where, what, how could I pursue those strange phonetic sounds that it was always said our African ancestor had spoken. It seemed obvious that I had to reach as wide a range of actual Africans as I possibly could, simply because so many different tribal tongues are spoken in Africa. There in New York City, I began doing what seemed logical: I began arriving at the United Nations around quitting time; the elevators were spilling out people who were thronging through the lobby on their way home. It wasn't hard to spot the Africans, and every one I was able to stop, I'd tell my sounds to. Within a couple of weeks, I guess I had stopped about two dozen Africans, each of whom had given me a quick look, a quick listen, and then took off. I can't say I blame them—me trying to communicate some African sounds in a Tennessee accent.

5 Increasingly frustrated, I had a long talk with George Sims, with whom I'd grown up in Henning, and who is a master researcher. After a few days, George brought me a list of about a dozen people academically renowned for their knowledge of African linguistics. One whose background intrigued me quickly was a Belgian, Dr. Jan Vansina. After study at the University of London's School of African and Oriental Studies, he had done

his early work living in African villages and written a book called *La Tradition Orale*. I telephoned Dr. Vansina where he now taught at the University of Wisconsin, and he gave me an appointment to see him. It was a Wednesday morning that I flew to Madison, Wisconsin, motivated by my intense curiosity about some strange phonetic sounds . . . and with no dream in this world of what was about to start happening. . . .

6   That evening in the Vansinas' living room, I told him every syllable I could remember of the family narrative heard since little boyhood—recently buttressed by Cousin Georgia in Kansas City. Dr. Vansina, after listening intently throughout, then began asking me questions. Being an oral historian, he was particularly interested in the physical transmission of the narrative down across generations.

7   We talked so late that he invited me to spend the night, and the next morning Dr. Vansina, with a very serious expression on his face, said, "I wanted to sleep on it. The ramifications of phonetic sounds preserved down across your family's generations can be immense." He said that he had been on the phone with a colleague Africanist, Dr. Philip Curtin; they both felt certain that the sounds I'd conveyed to him were from the "Mandinka" tongue. I'd never heard that word; he told me that it was the language spoken by the Mandingo people. Then he guess translated certain of the sounds. One of them probably meant cow or cattle; another probably meant the baobab tree, generic in West Africa. The word *ko*, he said, could refer to the *kora*, one of the Mandingo people's oldest stringed instruments, made of a halved large dried gourd covered with goatskin, with a long neck, and twenty-one strings with a bridge. An enslaved Mandingo might relate the *kora* visually to some among the types of stringed instruments that U.S. slaves had.

8   The most involved sound I had heard and brought was Kamby Bolongo, my ancestor's sound to his daughter Kizzy as he had pointed to the Mattaponi River in Spotsylvania County, Virginia. Dr. Vansina said that without question, *bolongo* meant, in the Mandinka tongue, a moving water, as a river; preceded by "Kamby," it could indicate the Gambia River.

9   I'd never heard of it.

10   An incident happened that would build my feeling—especially as more uncanny things occurred—that, yes, they were up there watchin' . . .

11   I was asked to speak at a seminar held at Utica College, Utica, New York. Walking down a hallway with the professor who had invited me, I said I'd just flown in from Washington and why I'd been there. "The Gambia? If I'm not mistaken, someone mentioned recently that an outstanding student from that country is over at Hamilton."

12   The old, distinguished Hamilton College was maybe a half hour's drive away, in Clinton, New York. Before I could finish asking, a Professor Charles Todd said, "You're talking about Ebou Manga." Consulting a course roster, he told me where I could find him in an agricultural economics class.

Ebou Manga was small of build, with careful eyes, a reserved manner, and black as soot. He tentatively confirmed my sounds, clearly startled to have heard me uttering them. Was Mandinka his home tongue? "No, although I am familiar with it." He was a Wolof, he said. In his dormitory room, I told him about my quest. We left for The Gambia at the end of the following week.

13   Arriving in Dakar, Senegal, the next morning, we caught a light plane to small Yundum Airport in The Gambia. In a passenger van, we rode into the capital city of Banjul (then Bathurst). Ebou and his father, Alhaji Manga—Gambians are mostly Moslem—assembled a small group of men knowledgeable in their small country's history, who met with me in the lounge of the Atlantic Hotel. As I had told Dr. Vansina in Wisconsin, I told these men the family narrative that had come down across the generations. I told them in a reverse progression, backward from Grandma through Tom, Chicken George, then Kizzy saying how her African father insisted to other slaves that his name was "Kin-tay," and repetitively told her phonetic sounds identifying various things, along with stories such as that he had been attacked and seized while not far from his village, chopping wood.

14   When I had finished, they said almost with wry amusement, "Well, of course 'Kamby Bolongo' would mean Gambia River; anyone would know that." I told them hotly that no, a great many people *wouldn't* know it! They showed a much greater interest that my 1760s ancestor had insisted his name was "Kin-tay." "Our country's oldest villages tend to be named for the families that settled those villages centuries ago," they said. Sending for a map, pointing, they said, "Look, here is the village of Kinte-Kundah. And not too far from it, the village of Kinte-Kundah Janneh-Ya."

15   Then they told me something of which I'd never have dreamed: of very old men, called *griots*, still to be found in the older back-country villages, men who were in effect living, walking archives of oral history. A senior *griot* would be a man usually in his late sixties or early seventies; below him would be progressively younger *griots*—and apprenticing boys, so a boy would be exposed to those *griots'* particular line of narrative for forty or fifty years before he could qualify as a senior *griot*, who told on special occasions the centuries-old histories of villages, of clans, of families, of great heroes. Throughout the whole of black Africa such oral chronicles had been handed down since the time of the ancient forefathers, I was informed, and there were certain legendary *griots* who could narrate facets of African history literally for as long as three days without ever repeating themselves.

16   Seeing how astounded I was, these Gambian men reminded me that every living person ancestrally goes back to some time and some place where no writing existed; and then human memories and mouths and ears were the only ways those human beings could store and relay information. They said that we who live in the Western culture are so conditioned to the

"crutch of print" that few among us comprehend what a trained memory is capable of.

17   Since my forefather had said his name was "Kin-tay"—properly spelled "Kinte," they said—and since the Kinte clan was old and well known in The Gambia, they promised to do what they could to find a *griot* who might be able to assist my search.

18   Back in the United States, I began devouring books on African history. It grew quickly into some kind of obsession to correct my ignorance concerning the earth's second-largest continent. It embarrasses me to this day that up to then my images about Africa had been largely derived or inferred from Tarzan movies and my very little authentic knowledge had come from only occasional leafings through the *National Geographic*. All of a sudden now, after reading all day, I'd sit on the edge of my bed at night studying a map of Africa, memorizing the different countries' relative positions and the principal waters where slave ships had operated.

19   After some weeks, a registered letter came from The Gambia; it suggested that when possible, I should come back. But by now I was stony broke—especially because I'd been investing very little of my time in writing.

20   Once at a *Reader's Digest* lawn party, cofounder Mrs. Dewit Wallace had told me how much she liked an "Unforgettable Character" I had written—about a tough old seadog cook who had once been my boss in the U.S. Coast Guard—and before leaving, Mrs. Wallace volunteered that I should let her know if I ever needed some help. Now I wrote to Mrs. Wallace a rather embarrassed letter, briefly telling her the compulsive quest I'd gotten myself into. She asked some editors to meet with me and see what they felt, and invited to lunch with them, I talked about nonstop for nearly three hours. Shortly afterward, a letter told me that the *Reader's Digest* would provide me with a three-hundred-dollar monthly check for one year, and plus that—my really vital need—"reasonable necessary travel expenses."

21   I again visited Cousin Georgia in Kansas City—something had urged me to do so, and I found her quite ill. But she was thrilled to hear both what I had learned and what I hoped to learn. She wished me Godspeed, and I flew then to Africa.

22   The same men with whom I had previously talked told me now in a rather matter-of-fact manner that they had caused word to be put out in the back country, and that a *griot* very knowledgeable of the Kinte clan had indeed been found—his name, they said, was "Kebba Kanji Fofana." I was ready to have a fit. "Where *is* he?" They looked at me oddly: "He's in his village."

23   I discovered that if I intended to see this *griot*, I was going to have to do something I'd never have dreamed I'd ever be doing—organizing what seemed, at least to me then, a kind of minisafari! It took me three days of negotiating through unaccustomed endless African palaver finally to hire a launch to get upriver; to rent a lorry and a Land-Rover to take supplies by a

roundabout land route; to hire finally a total of fourteen people, including three interpreters and four musicians, who had told me that the old *griots* in the back country wouldn't talk without music in the background.

24 In the launch *Baddibu,* vibrating up the wide, swift "Kamby Bolongo," I felt queasily, uncomfortably alien. Did they all have me appraised as merely another pith helmet? Finally ahead was James Island, for two centuries the site of a fort over which England and France waged war back and forth for the ideal vantage point to trade in slaves. Asking if we might land there awhile, I trudged amid the crumbling ruins yet guarded by ghostly cannon. Picturing in my mind the kinds of atrocities that would have happened there, I felt as if I would like to go flailing an ax back through that facet of black Africa's history. Without luck I tried to find for myself some symbol remnant of an ancient chain, but I took a chunk of mortar and a brick. In the next minutes before we returned to the *Baddibu,* I just gazed up and down that river that my ancestor had named for his daughter far across the Atlantic Ocean in Spotsylvania County, Virginia. Then we went on, and upon arriving at a little village called Albreda, we put ashore, our destination now on foot the yet smaller village of Juffure, where the men had been told that this *griot* lived.

25 There is an expression called "the peak experience"—that which emotionally, nothing in your life ever transcends. I've had mine, that first day in the back country of black West Africa.

26 When we got within sight of Juffure, the children who were playing outside gave the alert, and the people came flocking from their huts. It's a village of only about seventy people. Like most back-country villages, it was still very much as it was two hundred years ago, with its circular mud houses and their conical thatched roofs. Among the people as they gathered was a small man wearing an off-white robe, a pillbox hat over an aquiline-featured black face, and about him was an aura of "somebodiness" until I knew he was the man we had come to see and hear.

27 As the three interpreters left our party to converge upon him, the seventy-odd other villagers gathered closely around me, in a kind of horseshoe pattern, three or four deep all around; had I stuck out my arms, my fingers would have touched the nearest ones on either side. They were all staring at me. The eyes just raked me. Their foreheads were furrowed with their very intensity of staring. A kind of visceral surging or a churning sensation started up deep inside me; bewildered, I was wondering what on earth was this . . . then in a little while it was rather as if some full-gale force of realization rolled in on me: Many times in my life I had been among crowds of people, but never where *every one was jet black!*

28 Rocked emotionally, my eyes dropped downward as we tend to do when we're uncertain, insecure, and my glance fell upon my own hands' brown complexion. This time more quickly than before, and even harder, another gale-force emotion hit me: I felt myself some variety of a hybrid . . . I felt somehow impure among the pure; it was a terribly shaming feeling. About

then, abruptly the old man left the interpreters. The people immediately also left me now to go crowding about him.

29   One of my interpreters came up quickly and whispered in my ears, "They stare at you so much because they have never here seen a black American." When I grasped the significance, I believe that hit me harder than what had already happened. They hadn't been looking at me as an individual, but I represented in their eyes a symbol of the twenty-five millions of us black people whom they had never seen, who lived beyond an ocean.

30   The people were clustered thickly about the old man, all of them intermittently flicking glances toward me as they talked animatedly in their Mandinka tongue. After a while, the old man turned, walked briskly through the people, past my three interpreters, and right up to me. His eyes piercing into mine, seeming to feel I should understand his Mandinka, he expressed what they had all decided they *felt* concerning those unseen millions of us who lived in those places that had been slave ships' destinations—and the translation came: "We have been told by the forefathers that there are many of us from this place who are in exile in that place called America—and in other places."

31   The old man sat down, facing me, as the people hurriedly gathered behind him. Then he began to recite for me the ancestral history of the Kinte clan, as it had been passed along orally down across centuries from the forefathers' time. It was not merely conversational, but more as if a scroll were being read; for the still, silent villagers, it was clearly a formal occasion. The *griot* would speak, bending forward from the waist, his body rigid, his neck cords standing out, his words seeming almost physical objects. After a sentence or two, seeming to go limp, he would lean back, listening to an interpreter's translation. Spilling from the *griot's* head came an incredibly complex Kinte clan lineage that reached back across many generations: who married whom; who had what children; what children then married whom; then their offspring. It was all just unbelievable. I was struck not only by the profusion of details, but also by the narrative's biblical style, something like: "— and so-and-so took as a wife so-and-so, and begat . . . and begat . . . and begat . . ." He would next name each begat's eventual spouse, or spouses, and their averagely numerous offspring, and so on. To date things the *griot* linked them to events, such as "—in the year of the big water"—a flood—"he slew a water buffalo." To determine the calendar date, you'd have to find out when that particular flood occurred.

32   Simplifying to its essence the encyclopedic saga that I was told, the *griot* said that the Kinte clan had begun in the country called Old Mali. Then the Kinte men traditionally were blacksmiths, "who had conquered fire," and the women mostly were potters and weavers. In time, one branch of the clan moved into the country called Mauretania; and it was from Mauretania that one son of this clan, whose name was Kairaba Kunta Kinte—a *marabout*, or holy man of the Moslem faith—journeyed down

into the country called The Gambia. He went first to a village called Pakali N'Ding, stayed there for a while, then went to a village called Jiffarong, and then to the village of Juffure.

33   In Juffure, Kairaba Kunta Kinte took his first wife, a Mandinka maiden whose name was Sireng. And by her he begot two sons, whose names were Janneh and Saloum. Then he took a second wife; her name was Yaisa. And by Yaisa, he begot a son named Omoro.

34   Those three sons grew up in Juffure until they became of age. Then the elder two, Janneh and Saloum, went away and founded a new village called Kinte-Kundah Janneh-Ya. The youngest son, Omoro, stayed on in Juffure village until he had thirty rains—years—of age, then the took as his wife a Mandinka maiden named Binta Kebba. And by Binta Kebba, roughly between the years 1750 and 1760, Omoro Kinte begat four sons, whose names were, in the order of their birth, Kunta, Lamin, Suwadu, and Madi.

35   The old *griot* had talked for nearly two hours up to then, and perhaps fifty times the narrative had included some detail about someone whom he had named. Now after he had just named those four sons, again he appended a detail, and the interpreter translated—

36   "About the time the King's soldiers came"—another of the *griot's* time-fixing references—"the eldest of these four sons, Kunta, went away from his village to chop wood . . . and he was never seen again. . . ." And the *griot* went on with his narrative.

37   I sat as if I were carved of stone. My blood seemed to have congealed. This man whose lifetime had been in this back-country African village had no way in the world to know that he had just echoed what I had heard all through my boyhood years on my grandma's front porch in Henning, Tennessee . . . of an African who always had insisted that his name was "Kintay"; who had called a guitar a "*ko*," and a river within the state of Virginia, "Kamby Bolongo"; and who had been kidnaped into slavery while not far from his village, chopping wood, to make himself a drum.

38   I managed to fumble from my dufflebag my basic notebook, whose first pages containing grandma's story I showed to an interpreter. After briefly reading, clearly astounded, he spoke rapidly while showing it to the old *griot*, who became agitated; he got up, exclaiming to the people, gesturing at my notebook in the interpreter's hands, and *they* all got agitated.

39   I don't remember hearing anyone giving an order. I only recall becoming aware that those seventy-odd people had formed a wide human ring around me, moving counterclockwise, chanting softly, loudly, softly; their bodies close together, they were lifting their knees high, stamping up reddish puffs of the dust. . . .

40   The woman who broke from the moving circle was one of about a dozen whose infant children were within cloth slings across their backs. Her jet-black face deeply contorting, the woman came charging toward me, her bare feet slapping the earth, and snatching her baby free, she thrust it at me

almost roughly, the gesture saying "Take it!" . . . and I did, clasping the baby
to me. Then she snatched away her baby; and another woman was thrust-
ing her baby, then another, and another . . . until I had embraced probably
a dozen babies. I wouldn't learn until maybe a year later, from a Harvard
University professor, Dr. Jerome Bruner, a scholar of such matters, "You
didn't know you were participating in one of the oldest ceremonies of humankind, called 'The laying on of hands'! In their way, they were telling
you 'Through this flesh, which is us, we are you, and you are us!'"

41   Later the men of Juffure took me into their mosque built of bamboo and
thatch, and they prayed around me in Arabic. I remember thinking, down
on my knees, "After I've found out where I came from, I can't understand a
word they're saying." Later the crux of their prayer was translated for me:
"Praise be to Allah for one long lost from us whom Allah has returned."

42   Since we had come by the river, I wanted to return by land. As I sat beside the wiry young Mandingo driver who was leaving dust pluming behind us on the hot, rough, pitted, back-country road toward Banjul, there
came from somewhere into my head a staggering awareness . . . that *if* any
black American could be so blessed as I had been to know only a few ancestral clues—could he or she know *who* was either the paternal or maternal
African ancestor or ancestors, and about *where* that ancestor lived when
taken, and finally about *when* the ancestor was taken—then only those few
clues might well see that black American able to locate some wizened old
black *griot* whose narrative could reveal the black American's ancestral
clan, perhaps even the very village.

43   In my mind's eye, rather as if it were mistily being projected on a screen,
I began envisioning descriptions I had read of how collectively millions of
our ancestors had been enslaved. Many thousands were individually kidnaped, as my own forebear Kunta had been, but into the millions had come
awake screaming in the night, dashing out into the bedlam of raided villages, which were often in flames. The captured able survivors were linked
neck-by-neck with thongs into processions called "coffles," which were
sometimes as much as a mile in length. I envisioned the many dying, or left
to die when they were too weak to continue the torturous march toward the
coast, and those who made it to the beach were greased, shaved, probed in
every orifice, often branded with sizzling irons; I envisioned them being
lashed and dragged toward the longboats; their spasms of screaming and
clawing with their hands into the beach, biting up great choking mouthfuls
of the sand in their desperation efforts for one last hold on the Africa that
had been their home; I envisioned them shoved, beaten, jerked down into
slave ships' stinking holds and chained onto shelves, often packed so
tightly that they had to lie on their sides like spoons in a drawer. . . .

44   My mind reeled with it all as we approached another, much larger village. Staring ahead, I realized that word of what had happened in Juffure
must have left there well before I did. The driver slowing down, I could see
this village's people thronging the road ahead; they were waving, amid

their cacophony of crying out something; I stood up in the Land-Rover, waving back as they seemed grudging to open a path for the Land-Rover.

45   I guess we had moved a third of the way through the village when it suddenly registered in my brain what they were all crying out . . . the wizened, robed elders and younger men, the mothers and the naked tar-black children, they were all waving up at me; their expressions buoyant, beaming, all were crying out together, *"Meester Kinte! Meester Kinte!"*

46   Let me tell you something: I am a man. A sob hit me somewhere around my ankles; it came surging upward, and flinging my hands over my face, I was just bawling, as I hadn't since I was a baby. *"Meester Kinte!"* I just felt like I was weeping for all of history's incredible atrocities against fellowmen, which seems to be mankind's greatest flaw. . . .

47   Flying homeward from Dakar, I decided to write a book. My own ancestors' would automatically also be a symbolic saga of all African-descent people—who are without exception the seeds of someone like Kunta who was born and grew up in some black African village, someone who was captured and chained down in one of those slave ships that sailed them across the same ocean, into some succession of plantations, and since then a struggle for freedom.

48   In New York, my waiting telephone messages included that in a Kansas City Hospital, our eighty-three-year-old Cousin Georgia had died. Later, making a time-zone adjustment, I discovered that she passed away within the very hour that I had walked into Juffure Village. I think that as the last of the old ladies who talked the story on Grandma's front porch, it had been her job to get me to Africa, then she went to join the others up there watchin'.

49   In fact, I see starting from my little boyhood, a succession of related occurrences that finally when they all joined have caused this book to exist. Grandma and the others drilled the family story into me. Then, purely by the fluke of circumstances, when I was cooking on U.S. Coast Guard ships at sea, I began the long trial-and-error process of teaching myself to write. And because I had come to love the sea, my early writing was about dramatic sea adventures gleaned out of yellowing old maritime records in the U.S. Coast Guard's Archives. I couldn't have acquired a much better preparation to meet the maritime research challenges that this book would bring.

50   Always, Grandma and the other old ladies had said that a ship brought the African to "somewhere called 'Naplis." I knew they had to have been referring to Annapolis, Maryland. So I felt now that I had to try to see if I could find *what* ship had sailed to Annapolis from the Gambia River, with her human cargo including "the African," who would later insist that "Kintay" was his name, after his massa John Waller had given him the name "Toby."

51   I needed to determine a time around which to focus search for this ship. Months earlier, in the village of Juffure, the *griot* had timed Kunta Kinte's capture with "about the time the King's soldiers came."

52   Returning to London, midway during a second week of searching in records of movement assignments for British military units during the 1760s, I finally found that "King's soldiers" *had* to refer to a unit called "Colonel O'Hare's forces." The unit was sent from London in 1767 to guard the then British-operated Fort James Slave Fort in the Gambia River. The *griot* had been so correct that I felt embarrassed that, in effect, I had been checking behind him.

53   I went to Lloyds of London. In the office of an executive named Mr. R. C. E. Landers, it just poured out of me what I was trying to do. He got up from behind his desk and he said, "Young man, Lloyds of London will give you all of the help that we can." It was a blessing, for through Lloyds, doors began to be opened for me to search among myriad old English maritime records.

54   I can't remember any more exhausting experience than my first six weeks of seemingly endless, futile, day-after-day searching in an effort to isolate and then pin down a specific slave ship on a specific voyage, from within cartons upon cartons, files upon files of old records of thousands of slave-ship triangular voyages among England, Africa, and America. Along with my frustration, the more a rage grew within me the more I perceived to what degree the slave trade, in its time, was regarded by most of its participants simply as another major industry, rather like the buying, selling, and shipment of livestock today. Many records seemed never to have been opened after their original storage; apparently no one had felt occasion to go through them.

55   I hadn't found a single ship bound from The Gambia to Annapolis, when in the seventh week, one afternoon about two-thirty, I was studying the 1,023rd sheet of slave-ship records. A wide rectangular sheet, it recorded the Gambia River entrances and exits of some thirty ships during the years 1766 and 1767. Moving down the list, my eyes reached ship No. 18, and automatically scanned across its various data heading entries.

56   On July 5, 1767—the year "the King's soldiers came"—a ship named *Lord Ligonier,* her captain, a Thomas E. Davies, had sailed from the Gambia River, her destination Annapolis. . . .

57   I don't know why, but oddly my internal emotional reaction was delayed. I recall passively writing down the information, I turned in the records, and walked outside. Around the corner was a little tea shop. I went in and ordered a tea and cruller. Sitting, sipping my tea, it suddenly hit me that quite possibly that ship brought Kunta Kinte!

58   I still owe the lady for the tea and cruller. By telephone, Pan American confirmed their last seat available that day to New York. There simply wasn't time to go by the hotel where I was staying; I told a taxi driver, "Heathrow Airport!" Sleepless through that night's crossing of the Atlantic, I was seeing in my mind's eye the book in the Library of Congress, Washington, D.C., that I had to get my hands on again. It had a light brown

cover, with darker brown letters—*Shipping in the Port of Annapolis,* by Vaughan W. Brown.

59   From New York, the Eastern Airlines shuttle took me to Washington; I taxied to the Library of Congress, ordered the book, almost yanked it from the young man who brought it, and went riffling through it . . . and there it was, confirmation! The *Lord Ligonier* had cleared Annapolis' customs officials on September 29, 1767.

60   Renting a car, speeding to Annapolis, I went to the Maryland Hall of Records and asked archivist Mrs. Phebe Jacobsen for copies of any local newspaper published around the first week of October 1767. She soon produced a microfilm roll of the Maryland *Gazette.* At the projection machine, I was halfway through the October 1 issue when I saw the advertisement in the antique typeface: "JUST IMPORTED, In the ship *Lord Ligonier,* Capt. Davies, from the River Gambia, in Africa, and to be sold by the subscribers, in Annapolis, for cash, or good bills of exchange on Wednesday the 7th of October next, A Cargo of CHOICE HEALTHY SLAVES. The said ship will take tobacco to London on liberty at 6s. Sterling per ton." The advertisement was signed by John Ridout and Daniel of St. Thos. Jenifer.

61   On September 29, 1967, I felt I should be nowhere else in the world except standing on a pier at Annapolis—and I was; it was two hundred years to the day after the *Lord Ligonier* had landed. Staring out to seaward across those waters over which my great-great-great-great-grandfather had been brought, again I found myself weeping.

62   The 1766–67 document compiled at James Fort in the Gambia River had included that the *Lord Ligonier* had sailed with 140 slaves in her hold. How many of them had lived through the voyage? Now on a second mission in the Maryland Hall of Records, I searched to find a record of the ship's cargo listed upon her arrival in Annapolis—and found it, the following inventory, in old-fashioned script: 3,265 "elephants' teeth," as ivory tusks were called; 3,700 pounds of beeswax; 800 pounds of raw cotton; 32 ounces of Gambian gold; and 98 "Negroes." Her loss of 42 Africans en route, or around one-third, was average for slaving voyages.

63   I realized by this time that Grandma, Aunt Liz, Aunt Plus, and Cousin Georgia also had been *griots* in their own ways. My notebooks contained their centuries-old story that our African had been sold to "Massa John Waller," who had given him the name "Toby." During his fourth escape effort, when cornered he had wounded with a rock one of the pair of professional slave-catchers who caught him, and they had cut his foot off, "Massa John's brother, Dr. William Waller," had saved the slave's life, then indignant at the maiming, had bought him from his brother. I dared to hope there might actually exist some kind of an actual documenting record.

64   I went to Richmond, Virginia. I pored through microfilmed legal deeds filed within Spotsylvania County, Virginia, after September 1767, when the *Lord Ligonier* had landed. In time, I found a lengthy deed dated Septem-

ber 5, 1768, in which John Waller and his wife Ann transferred to William Waller land and goods, including 240 acres of farmland . . . and then on the second page, "and also one Negro man slave named Toby."

65   My God!

66   In the twelve years since my visit to the Rosetta Stone, I have traveled half a million miles, I suppose, searching, sifting, checking, crosschecking, finding out more and more about the people whose respective oral histories had proved not only to be correct, but even to connect on both sides of the ocean. Finally I managed to tear away from yet more researching in order to push myself into actually writing this book. To develop Kunta Kinte's boyhood and youth took me a long time, and having come to know him well, I anguished upon his capture. When I began trying to write of his, or all of those Gambians' slave-ship crossing, finally I flew to Africa and canvassed among shipping lines to obtain passage on the first possible freighter sailing from any black African port directly to the United States. It turned out to be the Farrell Lines' *African Star.* When we put to sea, I explained what I hoped to do that might help me write of my ancestor's crossing. After each late evening's dinner, I climbed down successive metal ladders into her deep, dark, cold cargo hold. Stripping to my underwear, I lay on my back on a wide rough bare dunnage plank and forced myself to stay there through all ten nights of the crossing, trying to imagine what did he see, hear, feel, smell, taste—and above all, in knowing Kunta, what things did he think? My crossing of course was ludicrously luxurious by any comparison to the ghastly ordeal endured by Kunta Kinte, his companions, and all those other millions who lay chained and shackled in terror and their own filth for an average of eighty to ninety days, at the end of which awaited new physical and psychic horrors. But anyway, finally I wrote of the ocean crossing—from the perspective of the human cargo.

♦ Understanding Each Other: Discussion Questions

1. What made Alex Haley decide to write *Roots?*
2. Outline the steps that Haley took to find Toby (Kunta Kinte).
3. What popular American magazine sponsored Haley's search for Toby? Describe the financial support Haley was given.
4. Where is The Gambia located?
5. What is a *griot?* What special skill does such a person possess? Do you have any figures like him in your culture? If so, describe them.
6. What was ironic about the timing of Cousin Georgia's death? What does the phrase "up there watchin'" mean?

7. What does Haley mean by "the Rosetta Stone"? What is its significance to Haley? What is the real Rosetta Stone important for? Do you have an object of significance of this kind in your country? If so, how would you describe it?
8. Why did Haley take passage on a freighter from Africa to the United States? Where did he sleep at night on the ship? Why did he do this?
9. What do the following phrases mean?

to be "stony broke"	the "laying on of hands"
to wish someone *Godspeed*	to be branded
"the peak experience"	professional slave catchers
aquiline-featured	ludicrously luxurious

10. Have you ever been part of a population census? How are census records kept in your home country?

♦ Interactive Grammar and Usage: Rules in Reflection

An effective way to develop your writing skills is to analyze the style of a good writer. In the passage excerpted below, Alex Haley chooses to use many verbs in their *-ing* form. Such a form conveys a sense of ongoing action and helps give the reader the feeling of being present in the episode. If you want to achieve the same effect, you need to remember that the use of *-ing* covers several different grammatical functions in English.

1. *Past Tense.* The *-ing* form can be part of a verb clause that describes a continuing action: *they were chanting.* This tells the reader that the action went on over a period of time in the past.

2. *Adjective.* The *-ing* form can also be used as an adjective: *the moving circle.* Here *moving* modifies *circle.* When an *-ing* form is used as an adjective, it can be changed into a clause introduced by a relative *that: the moving circle* becomes *the circle that moves.*

3. *Adverb.* Another use of the *-ing* form is to give more information about *how* the action of *another* verb is being carried out: *they formed a human ring, moving counterclockwise.* In this example, *moving counterclockwise* tells you more about the *manner* in which the human ring was formed. In this case, *moving counterclockwise* serves as an adverb and could have been joined to the sentence by a conjunction like *while: they formed a human ring while moving counterclockwise.*

4. *Pronoun Object.* In a fourth use of the *-ing* form, an entire sentence can be made to function as the *object* of the verb of another or "dominant" sentence: *I don't remember hearing anyone giving an order.* In this sentence, *hearing anyone giving an order* could be replaced with a noun or pronoun, as in *I don't remember it.*

5. *Subdominant Object Sentence.* Finally, a sentence serving as the object of the verb of another sentence could also be attached by the use of *that* followed by a subject and the verb: *I don't remember that I heard anyone giving an order.*

With a classmate, read the following passage and identify the underlined *-ing* phrases in terms of the five functions explained above (1 — past tense, 2 — adjective, 3 — adverb, 4 — pronoun object, 5 — subdominant object sentence).

I don't remember <u>hearing anyone giving an order</u>, I only recall <u>becoming</u>
    (1)   (2)
<u>aware</u> that those seventy-odd people had formed a wide human ring around me, <u>moving counterclockwise</u>, <u>chanting</u> softly, loudly, softly; their
                                     (3)   (4)
bodies close together, they <u>were lifting</u> their knees high, stamping up red-
                                          (5)
dish puffs of dust. . . .

The woman who broke from the <u>moving circle</u> was one of about a dozen
                                                     (6)
whose infant children were within cloth slings across their backs. Her jet-
black face <u>deeply contorting</u>, the woman came <u>charging toward me</u>, her
                      (7)   (8)

bare feet <u>slapping the earth</u>, and <u>snatching</u> her baby free, she thrust it at me
⁹   ¹⁰
almost roughly, the gesture <u>saying</u> "Take it!" . . . and I did, <u>clasping</u> the
¹¹   ¹²
baby to me. Then she snatched away her baby; and another woman <u>was</u>

<u>thrusting</u> her baby, then another, and another . . . until I had embraced
¹³
probably a dozen babies. I wouldn't learn until maybe a year later, from a

Harvard University professor, Dr. Jerome Bruner, a scholar of such matters,

"You didn't know you <u>were participating in</u> one of the oldest ceremonies of
¹⁴
humankind, called 'The <u>laying on</u> of hands'! In their way, they <u>were telling</u>
¹⁵   ¹⁶
you 'Through this flesh, which is us, we are you, and you are us!'"

Your Answers:

1.	9.
2.	10.
3.	11.
4.	12.
5.	13.
6.	14.
7.	15.
8.	16.

◆ Increasing Word Power: Vocabulary in Context

Working with a partner, decide on the meaning *in context* of each of the following words or phrases. Then look up each item in a good English-English dictionary. Does the context meaning of the word in the reading differ in any way from the dictionary's definition? If so, how did the context help you understand the meaning of the word as used in the passage?

Word	Meaning in This Context	Dictionary Definition
intrigue		
utter		
astonishment		
uncanny		
miraculous		
pursue		
renowned		
intense		
curiosity		
buttressed		

Word	Meaning in This Context	Dictionary Definition
intently		
ramifications		
soot		
tentatively		
quest		
chronicles		
devouring		
inferred		
palaver		
queasily		
atrocities		
remnant		
transcends		
hybrid		
flicking		
lineage		
thronging		
cacophony		
wizened		
flaw		
symbolic		
fluke		
myriad		
riffling		
archivist		
indignant		
maiming		
anguished		
ghastly		
shackled		

◆ Finding Your Own Voice: For Discussion and Writing

1. Discuss your reaction to Haley's search for his ancestors.
   Here are some questions to assist you in your analysis.

   Do you think that Haley's descriptions of scenes in Africa and of the slaving voyages are effective? What makes them so?

   The reading selection is taken from the end of Haley's book. Why do you think Haley *ends* his book with the story of how he decided to write *Roots?*

   What effect would presenting the search *first*—at the beginning of the book—have on a reader?

Why is it important to Haley to trace his ancestry?
In your culture, is it important to know your family lineage?

2. Analyze Alex Haley's style, looking particularly at his sentence structure and sentence length and at his use of rhetorical devices.

3. Write the story of *your* lineage, starting as far back in history as you can. Use all the library resources at hand. Write a narration, description, or exposition.

4. Perform the scenario "It's not your fault!" to bring your work with this chapter full circle. Your teacher may ask you to write an essay about the theme of this scenario, by yourself or with other students.

CHAPTER 2

Chinese American

♦ Listening to Each Other: Scenario

See Chapter 1 for instructions on how to perform a scenario.
   Prepare and perform the scenario "A fashion for now."

♦ Speaking Out: Debriefing Questions

1. Which character had the better arguments in the scenario?
2. Were any new vocabulary words or phrases used during the presentation of the scenario? If so, write them down and, working with a partner, guess the meaning of these words from the context of the action.
3. Have you or has someone you know had an experience similar to the one in the scenario? Did it involve clothing or some other aspect of a cultural tradition? How did you handle the situation? Was it resolved to the satisfaction of everyone involved?
4. With which character did you identify? Why?
5. If the scenario were played out again, would you change anything the players said or did? What would you change?

♦ Reaching Out: Suggestions for Further Activities

1. Reenact the scenario, letting the person who played the daughter now be the mother. What new insights does this role reversal give you into the conflict?

2. Most large American cities have a distinct section which is known as "Chinatown." Plan a visit to the nearest one. What kinds of things will you want to see and do? Afterward, compare your observations and experiences with those of your classmates. Be sure to discuss what you learned about Chinese culture during your visit.

3. Go to a library and find a book about the contributions of Chinese Americans to the growth and development of the United States. In which areas were and are the Chinese peoples' contributions *especially* significant?

4. The movie musical *Flower Drum Song* presents a poignant account of the clashes between the older and the younger generation in a Chinese family over maintaining traditional customs. If possible, view the film and identify the points of conflict; think about how you feel about what happens in the story. After you read the selection from *Chinatown Family*, decide whether you see any similarities in the family situations.

5. Write an essay based on the theme of the scenario and bring it into class for group work.

♦ Reading: From *Chinatown Family*, by Lin Yutang

Read the following selection, keeping in mind the scenario you have already experienced. It is always a good idea to have an English-English dictionary at hand when you read. A useful technique is to read the selection through quickly the first time, highlighting words or phrases that you think you need to look up. Then go back and do a more careful reading, looking up unfamiliar words.

CHAPTER 3

1

1   When Mother Fong first came to America, it was not as if she had not seen an American before. In the celluloid, she had seen Jean Harlow, Clara Bow, and a great many American beauties whom she greatly admired, as well as a few tough men with hair on their chests, like Wallace Beery, who frightened her. Tom and Eva knew them by name in Chinese. Their mother remembered only one actor, Barry Fitzgerald, who was known to her as "Fi-choy," though her later passion was William Bendix. She had seen Barry Fi-choy in a certain picture, then playing a minor role, and she liked him so much that she remembered his name above all the rest. "That is the good one," she said any time she saw her Fi-choy appear on the film, and then she would smile. There was something in Fi-choy's simplicity which struck her as eminently like the Chinese she knew and therefore was easily familiar. She could tell what Fi-choy was going to do; she could never tell what Jean Harlow or Wallace Beery was going to do.

2   She reflected therefore that there were foreigners she could not understand and others that she could. She did not know, when she came to America, whether she was going to meet many Wallace Beery's or many Fi-choy's. Among the women stars, she could not understand "those grown-up girls that do not wear trousers," but she could understand Ida Lupino. She had seen Ida Lupino in an English picture at Hong Kong. She was hoping that America was full of Fi-choy's and Lupino's.

3   The idea of having an American daughter-in-law had rather frightened her. She had prayed to God that she would not have one of those glamorous untrousered females for her daughter. As far as she knew, such females were everywhere strutting about in the streets, in homes, in hotel bars and lobbies, at swimming pools and on the beach. She had a fear of blondes; the fact that a woman's hair could be golden and her eyes blue was so fantastic that she gave up thinking. She had actually seen one American woman, the Irish wife of the missionary in her village, who had a carrottop and carried a kind of bronze flame on her head. Well, if it could be bronze, it could be gold, green, blue, purple, turquoise, or aquamarine. Moreover, there were several Catholic nuns in Canton who had blue eyes, though she could not see their hair. A load had fallen from her heart when she walked down the gangplank and was introduced to a girl with dark hair and dark eyes, who was her son's wife. She was not a glamorous untrousered female.

4   A sort of pantomime went on always in the kitchen. The mother-in-law could cook Chinese dishes and the American daughter-in-law could not. Therefore there was no question that the mother was the boss in the kitchen. Flora loved Chinese dishes, and she was curious to learn how the mother made Chinese gravy and prepared the mysterious chicken, called *sunfong gai,* which was roast chicken, yet more than roast chicken. So, by a natural law the mother became the chief and Flora the second cook.

5   The mother was a woman of steady temperament. Like her husband, she talked and moved slowly, steadily, and firmly. It seemed that everything was on a lower musical pitch, and the pauses were as long as the sentences themselves. Flora was a little gushing, and the mother thought that was because she was an American. The Americans talked so fast, or it sounded so in her ears. The mother could not speak a word of English, and the daughter spoke only a few dozen words of Chinese. It was surprising how you could get along with pantomime within the confines of a kitchen. It was a continual guessing game. If Flora was willing to guess and guess again, and the mother was not irritated at her guessing wrong, it could be a lot of fun. The mother was not irritated because Flora had black hair and was a white woman, for whom there was a kind of natural respect, and Flora was willing to guess and guess again because the very first night Loy had told her that his mother liked her very much. So it was a pantomime with smiles. Flora thought it quite a change from the time when she had

cooked alone and the kitchen was a place where one held communion with one's own soul—a change especially with Tom and Eva dashing out and in. It was a good thing, too, that one could not quarrel much in pantomime, not very well. You could sulk in pantomime, and you could breathe hard and communicate your impatience, but that was about all. No words said meant no words regretted. That is why no horse bears another horse a grudge for years.

6   But since the kitchen had been transformed into a school for learning Cantonese, with the most up-to-date direct method of teaching modern languages taught by an unquestioned native professor, it was not surprising that Flora picked up many words of the Cantonese language, which she promptly styled "hoi-polloi." If come was *loy*, open was *hoi*, drunk was *joy*, see was *toy*, vegetable was *choy*, and mustard plant was *koy choy*, then, obviously, the language was just hoi-polloi. All you needed to learn Cantonese was to keep the *oy* pattern (remember the night-club artist Joy Toy?) and sprinkle some *aps*, *ucks*, *ums*, *ongs*, and *eongs*, and boom these syllables up and down through the air like a balloon, and you could deceive a Cantonese into thinking that you were talking his dialect although it might not make sense. Flora was so enthusiastic over this discovery that she caught herself saying, "Look at the airplane in the skoy." Her husband was Loy, anyway.

7   Flora also learned her name in the family. When in the midst of a conversation in Cantonese she heard the word, *daisow*, she knew they were speaking about her. The *dai* being in the falling, and the *sow* in the rising tone, the word seemed to hit the ground solidly and then lift up with a snappy questioning tone so that the second syllable sounded very much like the English word *sour*.

8   "Why am I sour?" asked Flora of her husband.

9   "It means 'elder sister-in-law.' You are their *daisow*, as I am their *daiko*, the eldest brother."

10   That fixed her position in the family. Her husband and the parents called her Flora, but Tom and Eva were forbidden to call her that and addressed her as Daisow, and when the parents spoke of Flora to the children, they also called her Daisow because it identified her position in the family. Only Yiko, being fluent in American, preferred to call her Flora. Tom loved the name Flora so much that he asked one day, "Can I call you Flora?"

11   "Please do. Why not?"

"No, I guess I had better not."

But Tom continued to hear Yiko call Daisow, Flora. She was as much Yiko's elder sister-in-law as Tom's. Why couldn't he?

He asked his mother if he could call her Flora, and she said he could not. He asked his father, and he said he could not.

"Why can't I?"

"Because it is disrespectful. It shows no respect for your superior."

He asked Yiko.

"Yiko, you call Flora, Flora."

"I do."

"Can I call her Flora?"

"You can't."

"But why can you?"

"Because I am taller. I am taller and bigger than Daiko. I call her Flora. I call any American girl by her first name. But you are so small."

"Tell me, how do I say *put keng* in English?"

"You say 'no respect.' That is a common word. Do you want to learn some fine words?"

"Please tell me what I should say? I want to tell Flora why I don't call her by her name."

"If you want to use a fine word, you tell her it is because you don't want to be regardless. That means no regard. Or you say irrespective."

12   Tom learned the hard words and repeated them. Finding Flora alone, he came up and said, "Daisow, I have decided not to call you Flora."

13   "Why not? I don't mind."

"Because Father said it would be—"

"It would be what?"

"Because—because I don't want to be regardless and irrespective to you."

"What? Tom, you have learned long words!"

"Gee, I wish I could call you Flora. When I love a girl, I am going to call her Flora."

14   Flora kissed him on the head for that, and Tom dashed out of the kitchen.

2

15   For weeks Mrs. Fong would not budge again from her home. She was in her Chinese jacket and pants, and she would not be laughed at, and she was at an age when a complete change of her costume was unthinkable. Coming to this foreign country, her one guiding thought was that her family should be respected and honored among her neighbors. It was not a conscious thought; it was her whole attitude toward life that no one, including herself, should do anything to disgrace the family. That was all she asked of life and of America. No son should dishonor her in the eyes of her neighbors; it was a divine and ever present law of society that no one should "lose face" before his neighbors, a law more valid and binding on members of a community than all the codes and statutes. The punishment for viola-

tion of this invisible law of face was laughter and ridicule. And yet here she found herself in a ridiculous situation. She felt her dress should conform, and yet she could not conform, and how ridiculous it would be for her to put on a hat! She had seen women's hats, and all of them looked ridiculous enough, in fact, entirely laughable. She had seen how some elderly women in Chinatown made themselves so by putting on a hat and a long black dress covering the ankles, like that worn by the Salvation Army women, and she concluded that she would keep her dignity by keeping to her Chinese costume. At least she knew to dress in Chinese.

16   But it was not hard for her to stay at home. Women in China managed to stay in the house without going outdoors for months. She did not come to look at America; she came to be with her family. It was a surprise to her, however, that there were no such things as neighbors in New York City and that you hardly talked to the people next door or in the same building. That simplified matters for her since the family was left very much alone. Having no neighbors meant that one had no people before whom to lose face.

17   Often Mrs. Fong went to the window to survey the strange scene below and to watch Americans, men and women and children. In the mornings the street was quiet and clean. The sidewalks were cement, smooth like a house floor, and neat little garbage cans stood in groups before basement railings. Only a stone's throw away was Third Avenue, which was dark, noisy, and familiar. There was something about the darkness and familiarity and busyness of the avenue that she liked. She had never wanted to live in a deserted street, which meant that one was living in reduced circumstances. She had always wanted to live in a busy, prosperous thoroughfare, with lots of noise and people, and to be on the same footing with all the struggling millions. Third Avenue seemed to be just that. The shops—groceries, fruit stores, shoe-repair shops, upholstery shops, shops advertising men's two-pants suits, a supermarket—were all within half a minute's walk. Housewives with bags in their hands, fat women in black, young women in white and printed rayon, trucks, cars, horse carts selling fresh vegetables, barrel organs, all passed the corner in continuous procession. Up above, at five-minute intervals, trains carrying loads of people dashed past, swiftly, securely. All this rumble, this intense activity of people going somewhere, gave her a sense of excitement and of being in the midst of things. Where there were plenty of people in a city such as New York, she was sure there was money to be made. No wonder her husband had been able to send dollars home. Take laundry. There was so much to be washed in that one block alone. Her husband had spoken of washing America and cooking America. She needed only to wash the block, and perhaps, in the not impossible future, cook to feed the block. After eating American food on the ship, she was not surprised that the Chinese took to cooking for Americans. As she sat before the window, the conviction grew in her mind

that there was plenty of money to be made in New York, and she was going to make it.

18   Yet there were "face" and disgrace even in this street of anonymous neighbors. As she watched out of the window and saw housewives emerge from this or that house, she could see which were neat and nice women and which were lazy, sloppy housewives. In this neighborhood known as Yorkville there were many Germans and Czechs, but all nationalities were mixed. There was a sweet young Belgian woman whose blond hair was always done up in a queue would neatly round her head, an old Bulgarian woman whose white hair was gathered up simply in a tiny bun at the back, and there was a fat woman whose enormous outlines were casually covered by a dress that showed no recognizable difference from a nightgown or a sack with a V-shaped opening at the top.

19   Toward three in the afternoon the street suddenly sprang into life. Children appeared playing, chopping wooden boxes, skipping rope, roller-skating, playing cop and gangster, chasing, running, and screaming. Grown-up girls of sixteen or seventeen were not ashamed to be seen skating on the sidewalks like little children. Mother Fong surveyed it all. Clearly, there were face and disgrace. From the Idle Hour Tavern at the corner she saw drunken men, filthy and besotted, emerge staggering to stand or crouch on the sidewalk in various stages of intoxication. The young girls in the streets were prettily dressed, walking head up at a pace that sent their golden hair flopping up and down around the nape. It was the characteristically American gait. Before the third house, where the sloppy woman lived, a group of small children were playing. They looked filthy, and she was sure they were the children of the woman who looked like a drudge. Her guess was correct, because a few days later she saw the woman come out and spank the girl before she literally dragged her in.

20   Her idea of face was that she would never allow Tom and Eva to appear that way in the street. American clothes for boys and girls were pretty, and they looked well on Tom and Eva. Mother Fong admired the girls' ringlets, and Flora knew how to make them, so within a week Eva had said good-by to her pigtails. Even though other girls wore pigtails, she would never wear them again. As for Tom, as long as he could remember, the fortnightly Saturday haircut at the Lexington Avenue barber shop was a sacred and inviolable institution. His head was cropped clean and close at the back, and a small wisp of hair always fell across one side of his forehead.

21   "Look like a gentleman," the mother said. "We are Chinese, and you do not want to disgrace China."

22   Regularly at four o'clock the mother dressed them up, Tom with his hair parted and his neck scrubbed, and Eva with her pretty ringlets and a clean cotton dress. It is to be suspected that some advertisement tactics were involved. Clean children should emerge from a clean laundry. Were Tom and

Eva to be walking signboards of Tom Fong's Hand Laundry? Mother Fong reasoned that people would not send their laundry to a place where the children looked as filthy as those in the third house opposite. Or was it a code of honor for a laundryman's son that his shirt should be superiorly clean, like a professor's son who is not permitted to say "he ain't" while other children do?

23   The children were not yet at school, and the mother had decided that they needed exercise. Regularly at four o'clock they had to go out of the house somewhere, no matter where. After staring at their eyes and noses for unclean spots until Tom felt the dirt would pop out of his nose if there was any, the mother commanded, "Now, Tom and Eva, march!"

24   "Where to, Mother?"

"To the Central Park. It is good for you."

"We were there yesterday," Eva protested.

"Never mind where you go. Now, march!"

25   Tom and Eva marched forward, past the toilet at the end of the hallway, down the staircase, and out into the street. Their mother's head was always at the window, and Tom and Eva always looked up and smiled, though sometimes, to their disappointment, their mother was already looking away.

26   Eva hated this marching business. At the corner, the question was always, "Where?" The East River and Central Park were approximately the same distance away and equally obnoxious. Eva liked the park well enough, but crossing the wide Park Avenue was always an exciting and trying adventure. Once arrived at the park, Eva and Tom enjoyed it, Eva usually holding Tom's hand until they decided on a spot. She did not care for romping about, it was so childish and unwomanly. Boys should romp about; girls should not. So she often sat on one of the benches, guarding her ringlets and swaying her legs for exercise.

27   Third Avenue was a universe. From Seventieth Street to Ninetieth, bounded by Second Avenue on one side and Lexington on the other, the district was a universe for Tom's exploration. He reconnoitered it, played and worked and walked in it, tasted it, smelled it, swam in it like a whirling planet until he could recognize the very air he breathed. The smell of the Eighties was different from the smell of the Sixties, and he could shut his eyes and tell in which he was. Third Avenue was longer than the longest street in his home town, and the El seemed to cross its orbit and swim out of his ken into infinity. Only a few blocks away, he would come to the different and bright business district of Eighty-sixth Street, where neon lights and illuminated signs glared in competition from four movie theaters within a block of each other. Out on Lexington the vibrations were again different. Second Avenue seemed like a suburban district where there was more air and sunlight and the population moved on what was the periphery of this tense, exciting, brooding universe.

28   It was a little universe in itself in which babies were born, food was eaten, laxatives were taken, and the dead were embalmed, completing the life process. Several funeral parlors in the district attested to this last fact. A city hermit, choosing to live like a hermit crab, could live in one of these blocks and never go outside for what he wanted. Boys grew up and fought and burned wooden boxes in the street to melt the snow in winter and dashed almost naked through the water from the hydrant in summer, grown-up boys and girls had dates in dark doorways, and men toiled and sweated, and women scrubbed and cooked, and the old sat on the doorsteps in summer evenings. It teemed with life, and on summer nights it was wet with the perspiration of humanity.

from Lin Yutang. *Chinatown Family*, 1948. By permission of Taiyi Lin Lai and Hsiang Ju Lin.

◆ Understanding Each Other: Discussion Questions

1. Are you or is anyone you know married to an American? How did your family (or that family) react to the news of your marriage? Does everyone involved feel comfortable with the situation now?
2. Describe the relationship between Mother Fong and Flora, her American daughter-in-law. Give evidence from the story to support your description.
3. What Chinese traditions are maintained in the Loy household? Do you know people of Chinese descent? If so, what can they tell you about their family traditions?
4. What is a *celluloid*? Who were Jean Harlow, Clara Bow, Wallace Beery, Barry Fitzgerald, William Bendix, and Ida Lupino? Have you ever seen them perform?
5. Describe the colors *bronze*, *purple*, *turquoise*, and *aquamarine*.
6. Why do you think that Yiko is allowed to call Flora by her American name?
7. How does Tom feel about Flora? Cite evidence from his speech and actions to support your answer.
8. In paragraph 13, when Tom explains to Flora why he had decided *not* to call her "Flora," he says it's "because I don't want to be regardless and irrespective to you." What does *regardless* really mean? *Irrespective*? What words should he have used here?
9. How important is maintaining face and family honor to Mother Fong? Is maintaining face important in your culture? What about in other cultures that you know about?
10. What is the Salvation Army?

11. Describe the neighborhood in which the Loy family lives. What kinds of activities go on there? What is the *El?* A *hydrant?*

12. What do the following phrases mean?

dashing in and out   living in reduced circumstances
in the midst of   a prosperous thoroughfare
basement railings   to be on the same footing with
a stone's throw   neon lights

♦ Interactive Grammar and Usage: Rules in Reflection

With a partner, fill in the blanks with appropriate articles, adjectives, or adverbs. Your teacher may give you a list of choices. Your goal is to make the passage both coherent and cohesive. You should put in the words that strike you as contributing most to its overall coherence. After filling in all the blanks, go back and reread the passage, making any changes in the words selected in order to improve its internal cohesiveness. You will note that some of the choices are those found in the reading; others are close in meaning. Be prepared to explain the reason for each answer that you select. The first sentence is done for you.

Often Mrs. Fong went to the window to survey the strange scene below and to watch Americans, men and women and children. In _____
mornings the street was _____ and _____ . The sidewalks were cement, _____ like a _____ floor, and _____ _____ garbage cans stood in groups before basement railings. _____ a stone's throw away was Third Avenue, which was dark, _____ ,and _____ . There was something about the darkness and familiarity and busyness of the avenue that she liked. She had _____ wanted to live in a _____ street, which meant that one was living in reduced circumstances. She had _____ wanted to live in a _____ , prosperous thoroughfare, with lots of noise and people, and to be on the _____ footing with all the struggling millions. . . . Housewives with bags in _____ hands, fat women in black, _____ women in white and _____ rayon, trucks, cars, horse carts selling _____ vegetables, barrel organs, all passed _____ corner in _____ procession. Up _____ , at five-minute intervals, trains carrying loads of people dashed past, _____ , securely. All this rumble, this _____ activity of people going somewhere, gave her _____ sense of excitement and of being in the midst of things.

♦ Increasing Word Power: Vocabulary in Context

Working with a partner, decide on the meaning *in context* of each of the following words or phrases. Then look up each item in a good English-English dictionary. Does the context meaning of the word in the reading differ in any way from the dictionary's definition? If so, how did the context help you understand the meaning of the word as used in the passage?

Word	Meaning in This Context	Dictionary Definition
eminently		
glamorous		
strutting		
missionary		
carrottop		
nuns		
gangplank		
pantomime		
mysterious		
temperament		
gushing		
communion		
soul		
sulk		
transformed		
snappy		
budge		
disgrace		
divine		
ridicule		
dignity		
survey		
anonymous		
sloppy		
queue		
besotted		
crouch		
flopping		
drudge		
inviolable		
reconnoitered		
whirling		
ken		
periphery		
brooding		
laxatives		
embalmed		
hermit		
teemed		
perspiration		

◆ Finding Your Own Voice: For Discussion and Writing

1. The excerpt you read from Lin Yutang's book is full of vivid descriptions of New York City. Choose *two* paragraphs from the reading and, imitating her style (that is, using the same sentence structure and word forms that she uses), write a description of your own hometown neighborhood.

2. Think about the traditions and customs of your own family. Have they changed from your grandparents' time to today? The list below presents some matters that pertain to family life. Check off the similarities and differences, and prepare to tell the class about the changes that have occurred in your family.

	Same	**Different**
Family celebrations		
Adherence to religious rites or practices		
The language used to talk to *older* members of the family, including parents, aunts, and uncles		
The language used to talk to *younger* relatives, including brothers, sisters, and cousins		

3. Perform the scenario "A matter of taste" to bring your work with this chapter full circle. Your teacher may ask you to write an essay with other students about one aspect of the scenario.

German American

◆ Listening to Each Other: Scenario

See Chapter 1 for instructions on how to perform a scenario.
Prepare and perform the scenario "Privacy."

◆ Speaking Out: Debriefing Questions

1. Discuss the reactions of the two spouses in the scenario. How did they solve their dilemma?
2. What solution or solutions did the relative offer?
3. Did the fact that the relative's family own a dog and a rabbit complicate matters?
4. How important to each of the characters in the scenario was the issue of privacy and the protection of property? How important are these things in your native culture? To you personally?
5. Are there any other possible solutions to this problem? And would you change anything if the scenario were acted out again?

◆ Reaching Out: Suggestions for Further Activities

1. Poll your classmates or a group outside of class on the issue of privacy. Do you find any differences in points of view based on age? On gender? On education?

2. Every ten years, the federal government of the United States takes a census. This survey is done not only to count the population but also to update programs and benefits which serve Americans. Get a copy of the most recent U.S. census from your city library or local government office and interview a classmate, using the census questions. How did that person react to the questions? How do you feel about the questions? Are they acceptable, or do you think they invade your privacy?

3. The following is one role of a scenario. Complete the other role. Remember that each role in a scenario has the following elements: (1) some general information shared by all participants; (2) some particular information for each role player; and (3) a task to be completed, a goal to be attained, or a problem to be solved. After you have written your role, give it to the teacher, who will evaluate it and correct it, if necessary. If there is time, the teacher will ask some students to play the role you have written, while others will play the role that is given below.

   Waiter in a restaurant: The boss has told you to play a cassette tape of background music while the customers are having dinner. A good friend of yours has composed some music and has asked you to play it so that an agent might hear it and offer your friend a contract to publish it. The agent, who works with an important music-publishing firm, is eating his dinner while you play the music. He hears it and calls you over to speak to him about it. What will you tell him?

   Music-publishing agent: You are having your dinner in a restaurant. . . . Finish the scenario. In doing this exercise, you might find it helpful to think about answers to the following questions:

   Does the music agent find the music agreeable?
   Does he want to hear music this evening?
   Is it disturbing him? If so, why?

4. German Americans have played a major role in the development of American culture. H. L. Mencken and Theodore Dreiser are two prominent Americans of German extraction. Find out where they lived and what contributions they made.

5. Write an essay about the theme of one of the scenarios you have performed and then polish it with the help of your classmates.

◆ Reading: From *"Surviving" and Other Essays*, by Bruno Bettelheim

Read the following selection, keeping in mind the scenario you have already experienced. It is always a good idea to have an English-English dictionary at hand when you read. A useful technique is to read the selection through quickly the first time, highlighting words or phrases you think you need to look up. Then go back and do a more careful reading, looking up unfamiliar words.

SOME COMMENTS ON PRIVACY

1 When contemplating the issues raised by an ever more frequent, pervasive, and intrusive invasion of privacy by governmental agencies, private organizations, and the mass media—aggravated by requests from researchers for all kinds of detailed information on one's activities, opinions, and preferences—I am motivated by my considerable personal need and liking for privacy, and my resentment when it is infringed upon. I even dislike intensely what appear to be quite innocuous invasions of my private domain, unless I happen to be momentarily in the mood where it makes no difference to me. For example, there are times when I am quite annoyed if I have to listen to some music in an elevator or airplane, because it may jar with my mood of the moment, stop me from pursuing private thoughts, or interfere with a conversation. While petty, such incidents are indicative of a much larger issue: the usurpation of my right to decide whether, and if so, where I should listen to music, and what kind of music this should be. The fact that it is an anonymous organization which has made these decisions for me only makes it worse; while I am involved as an individual, there is no other individual to whom I can complain about the music, or ask for redress.

2 What I resent is not the music per se; even as I am disturbed by it, I recognize that it was arranged with the good intention of entertaining me while I am forced to spend time in a dull place. What bothers me is the tacit assumption either that I have no private thoughts I wish to pursue without interruption, or that these thoughts can easily be fitted to the mood of the music, or most offensive of all, that my wish to engage in thoughts of my own need not be respected.

3 I cite a trivial example because I believe privacy to be an unqualified right. The same principle that one's privacy should be respected and inviolate should apply in minor areas like elevators as well as in major ones such as one's professional life. As a psychoanalyst I am the recipient of highly confidential information about people's most intimate affairs, and not just from patients suffering from severe psychological disturbances. I am frequently subjected to the demand that I divulge this information. Although I reject such requests, to do so is often made very difficult. With all this, I would make a forceful case that privacy must be safeguarded under all circumstances, especially against any infringements by the power of the state. This conviction has been strengthened by my experiences with totalitarian systems.

4   However, I recognize how much my attitudes were formed in a particular era—the late- and post-Victorian one—and how much things have changed since that time. Reflecting on how things are now, I began to feel not just old, but outright archaic. I have had to accept that privacy is not universally desired, nor an absolute good, as I wished to believe. Instead, its high valuation belongs very much to a particular style of life and historical period, is further characteristic of certain social classes, and thus is culture-bound.

5   The troublesome nature of this divergence of attitudes began to dawn upon me as I was typing the first draft of these remarks, in solitude, the door of my room closed, in the stillness of the night—the time when I prefer working and when I work best, because no unexpected interruptions interfere with my concentration. As I was typing away, my eyes strayed to a favorite picture hung on the wall over the desk, and I had to laugh at myself. The picture was a copy of a famous painting by Pieter Breughel the Elder, a master I greatly admire. I particularly like this painting of his because it seems to me to be a celebration of life as it really is, not as it pretends to be, as is often rendered in pictures. It shows a world teeming with people, doing all sorts of things. A crowd is depicted who, singly or in groups, are unconcernedly, even happily, going about in public what I, from my very different perspective, would have called their private business. Only for them, such affairs were not at all private—on the contrary. They were fully aware that they transacted their interactions in public; they wanted all to be seen and known by neighbors and strangers; and they did things with more gusto because they did them in the presence of others who reacted to the events being carried on in their presence. I had enjoyed and admired this and other paintings of the Dutch masters, many of which depicted the most "private" aspects of life as being transacted in the public domain, without recognizing that my admiration was incompatible with my feelings about the desirability of privacy. These paintings and many others from later periods indicate how recently our need for privacy has developed; and as I reflected on it, I also realized that this need may already be passing out of our life.

6   When I studied as a youngster, the door to my room had to be closed; all had to be quiet, and was quiet. Only then could I concentrate on my thoughts and my work, to the exclusion of all other distractions. But my own children—the generation born during and after World War II—studied best with the door open and the record player or the radio going full blast; in this radically different setting they learned as much and as well as I had. Why then do I still need a high degree of privacy and have to work—or at least much prefer to work—only in quiet concentration; and why do they—like the people in the Breughel painting—need to be in continuous close touch with their age-mates, or at least symbolically through a shared musical interest, when they want to concentrate on a mentally demanding task?

7   Maybe the answer is that we all function best when we feel in communion with what seems to symbolize our highest personal value. I, as a child of the Victorian age, had to create for myself a setting that emphasized privacy, personal uniqueness, and individual development before I could concentrate on a learning task whose ultimate goal—whether or not I was consciously aware of it—was to attain the highest possible degree of individuation. My children, in order to work best, needed to feel that they had not lost touch with their peer group. Nothing and nobody forced them to accept the intrusion of the music into the privacy of their thoughts. If anything, their parents, who were the "authorities" in the home, were most dubious about their studying with the songs of the Beatles distracting them—or at least we thought that this loud music must distract them.

8   Actually, far from distracting, the music helped my children to concentrate by comforting and reassuring them that they had not lost contact with what they needed most. It gave them the feeling that even when immersed in their studies, they were still somehow in touch with what counted for much in their lives: the connection to their age group. This connection heightened life for them in all of their doings, including the effort to study.

9   The more lonely they felt, the more these children needed to deny their isolation, to drown it out by the loudness of the music. It expressed for them their angers, their longings, even their loneliness. In doing so, the loud music did for them what they felt unable to do for themselves: to bring their emotions into some semblance of order, put them into a frame which would make them manageable enough to be expressed; emotions which otherwise would be much too chaotic to be coped with in any way. This vicarious expression of their feelings by the music permitted the children—who hardly listened to it but let themselves be enveloped by it—to continue with their studies; otherwise the pressure of these feelings might have prevented them from doing so. The music did this for them because they knew their age-mates who suffered from overpowering parallel emotions listened to the same music. Thus even in their anger, their alienation, their loneliness, it established an invisible—I am tempted to say, an audible—imaginary bond between them and those others with whom, alas, no real bonds existed.

10   When I came to this country about thirty years ago, among the many customs which struck me as different and thus strange was having the window shades pulled down halfway, more or less all the time. The lowered shade signified a wish for privacy, while leaving half of the window unobstructed expressed that there was no desire, nor any need, to hide from inspection what went on in the room behind the window. This seemed to me to bespeak a strange ambivalence about the wish for privacy. Now the picture window, which exposes so much more of what goes on in the inside to outside scrutiny, while at the same time permitting insiders to

observe so much of what is going on in front of the window, has more or less done away with half-pulled-down shades.

11   In comparison, I remembered how the same problem of seeing and being seen through a window was often dealt with in my native Vienna, and in many other European countries. In the generation of my grandparents, many homes had one window of the living room fitted with an outside mirror that was angled so that a person sitting inside, in a window seat specially fitted for this purpose, could spy on all the comings and goings in the street by watching the mirror without being observed.

12   I could not help reflecting that a situation where one person would sit hidden in semi-obscurity while observing the behavior of others had its similarities with the psychoanalytic setting, where things go on in utter privacy and confidentiality. If so, the semi-private and semi-public nature of the partly pulled-down shade, and the more public exposure inherent in the picture window, might then be likened to group therapeutic settings or encounter groups, where a mixed group of patients and therapist are equally exposed to each other and things can barely be kept private or confidential. Maybe there were some deeper reasons why a setting that was typically Victorian in its insistence on maintaining total privacy and confidentiality was conducive to the invention of psychoanalysis, and with this to the liberation from Victorian hypocrisy.

13   How things have changed since Freud explained his reasons for developing the particular psychoanalytic setting! He created it because people, he felt, could not be expected to talk about sexual or other "private" matters while they were aware that somebody was observing their face. But the setting protected the analyst equally: sitting behind the couch where the patient could not observe him was absolutely necessary for the analyst, if he was to be able to concentrate on the patient and what he was saying without worrying about any expressions which might appear on *his* face as he listened to the patient's revelations.

14   But since Freud's time, and to a considerable degree because of his influence, what used to be eminently private has become quite public—often, I feel defensively, with a vengeance. Feelings and actions a patient could talk about only to the trusted analyst in the carefully guarded privacy of the treatment room are now freely discussed in public, with relative strangers and in the most casual settings. Questions which once a patient broached to his analyst only with great anxiety are now asked in widely and indiscriminately disseminated questionnaires and are readily answered, although they pertain to matters which I still believe ought best to be kept private. What used to be considered most intimate matters are now discussed in great detail in family magazines or shown on the TV or movie screen.

15   This greater openness, as concerning sexual matters for example, has not altered the fact that today, as in Freud's time, there is much a person

will not disclose unless he is absolutely certain that his confidences will be kept secret; but the content of what needs to be kept private has changed. For example, it used to be that the revelation of a person's sexual predilections—ordinary or deviant—had to be protected by complete confidentiality before he dared open up about them. Today many people speak freely about such matters in public. What now is kept secret is often a person's true feelings about behavior which he openly flaunts; feelings which may be the opposite of those he claims to have, for he may secretly be ashamed of what he so openly admits to, or, contrary to his assertions, he may not be able to feel at all.

16   Thus today, as much as in Freud's time, people insist on confidentiality and on keeping things private, whenever they are ashamed of what they have to reveal. What people may be ashamed of can and does change radically from place to place, and over time. This poses the psychological problem of whether such shame—and with it the demand for confidentiality and privacy—is desirable and beneficial, or rather lessens our well-being as individuals, or that of man in society. Do we benefit more when we are able to hide, keep private and secret, that of which we are ashamed, or is it preferable that this should be made public and openly accepted?

17   Here the psychoanalyst is caught in his own contradictions, like the rest of us. He tells his patients that there is nothing to be ashamed of in fantasies and feelings, not to mention dreams and daydreams. All these flow of necessity from one's total life history, from the vagaries of experiences and one's reactions to them. Most of all, they reflect early childhood events and reactions, and how one then immaturely interpreted the world; there is no reason for anybody to feel shame about such things. Yet when the same patient behaves in society too openly by acting on the basis of these fantasies, when he thus makes public things he has been told not to shrink from, then as likely as not, the psychoanalyst will consider such openness as acting-out on the part of the patient, viewing it as irresponsible and self-destructive behavior—which indeed it may be.

18   We all seem caught between our own morality and society's clamor about what should be kept private, and what not. So we all end up functioning by a double standard of morality. But as Freud has shown, keeping a double moral standard—maintaining one for public show and another for private and somehow shameful action—leads only to neurosis and hysteria. Maybe our present dilemma regarding what belongs in the private domain and what in the public, although different from the double standard of Freud's day, is caused by equally severe unresolved inner conflicts about what is right and what wrong.

19   As a Freudian psychoanalyst I cannot help one further reflection: that the genitals are called a person's private parts, and that the place where one defecates is called a privy. Behind these two "private" designations lies a

discomfort with natural functions, a distrust concerning basic parts of oneself, and an uneasiness about how others feel about such things—in short, a deep inner conflict.[1] Maybe these are the emotions behind many demands for privacy.

20   Lewis Mumford writes: "Today the degradation of the inner life is symbolized by the fact that the only place sacred from intrusion is the private toilet."[2] In this connection it might be mentioned that organizations which wish to de-individualize the individual insist on the use of common toilets, such as in the army, or in summer camps, where the desire is to make everybody feel like "one of the boys." This underlines the relation between individualism and privacy on the one hand, and on the other that between feelings of communality and absence of privacy. (Deliberate deprivation of all privacy can be used not only for purposes of de-individualization, but also of degradation and depersonalization, as happened in the concentration camps.)

21   Now the degradation Mumford talks of can be interpreted in two ways. One is the thought Mumford had in mind: that unfortunately too little in our lives is as private, as safe from intrusion, as we are while we are on the toilet. But is it not also degrading that functions so natural to our bodies, eliminatory functions we cannot live without, are considered so shameful that they have to be carefully hidden from others, and avoided through lingual circumlocution even with ourselves?

22   It is precisely the feelings we experience around toilet training, or what is called anality, that often become the greatest source of neurotic anxieties; our inherited shame about elimination sometimes forces us to keep shameful and guilty feelings private and hidden from others, causing tremendous unhappiness. At the same time, this very shame is one of the foundations on which our Western civilization rests, although along with it came the discomfort Freud wrote about which bedevils modern man.

23   Nevertheless in other areas, when and where we crave privacy has undergone great change. My Victorian parents, when they went out to dinner, preferred a spacious restaurant with their table set off by an ample distance from the next one. Conversation would then not be overheard, nor their attention imposed on or distracted by too immediate an awareness of others. Nowadays our young people seem to prefer to crowd together in small discotheques, not to speak of the hippies who sleep many to a room. Many of

---

[1]As openly as many people now talk about sexual matters, when it comes to elimination we still talk about "going to the bathroom," or washroom. Elimination is still "dirty." The shame about this finds expression in our circumlocution as we refer not to elimination, but instead to that which will free us from having been engaged in something we consider "dirty"—washing and cleaning ourselves.

[2]Lewis Mumford, *The City in History* (New York: Harcourt, Brace & World, 1961).

the latter feel so desperately alone and out of contact with others that bodily closeness is sought avidly to bridge the gap. This raises the problem of whether parents have not gone too far in their demand for and in their imposition of privacy.

24   One need not go as far back as when whole families lived in one room. Nobody had privacy then. One couldn't effectively hide certain skeletons in the closet then because there were no closets. Reconstructions of what life was like in colonial days, even among the affluent, show that parents and children alike lived not only physically close, but with hardly any privacy. A family had to be quite well off to afford separate bedrooms—that is, one for the parents, and one for all the children together. Nowadays the ideal seems to be for each child to have his own room and own bathroom. But the children raised in this spacious isolation are often those who, when they finally come into their own, crowd together into one tiny room.

25   Our Western society has gone far in seeking privacy and avoiding the pains of closeness; at least as an ideal, although many poor people cannot afford the luxury of privacy, which they desire. On the other hand, many who can afford privacy in consequence suffer from too much distance, from isolation. Maybe what we view as the infringement of privacy today has to do with human efforts at rectifying the balance.

26   Mumford writes that

the first radical change which was to alter the form of the Medieval house, was the development of a sense of privacy. This means in effect withdrawal at will from the common life and the common interests of one's fellows. Privacy in sleep, privacy in eating, privacy in religious and social rituals, finally privacy in thought. . . . The desire for privacy marked the beginning of that new alignment of classes which was to usher in the merciless class competition and individual self-assertion of a later day. . . . In the castles of the thirteenth century, one notes the existence of a private bedroom for the noble owners; and one also finds, not far from it, perched over the moat, a private toilet. . . . Privacy in bed came first in Italy among the upper classes only, but the desire for it seems to have developed almost as slowly as the means. Michelangelo, for example, on occasion slept with his workmen four to a bed.

27   From these remarks it seems obvious that an absence of privacy in living conditions did not and need not interfere with creative achievements, which even we moderns regard as the reflection of rarest uniqueness. But it also appears that as long as all the bodily functions, including sex and elimination, were more or less public, no great shame attached to them. Only as

they became more and more relegated to a private room which became the privy, did we learn to feel shame about our bodies and bodily functions. The tragedy is that alienation from one's body leads to alienation from oneself and from others. And once we no longer feel comfortable with others, we crave privacy. Maybe what is missing is the right balance between closeness and distance, between public and private.

28   When we think about privacy we think of the wish for privacy in thought, feeling, and experience; these should be exclusively our own. No one should have the right to intrude on these inner processes; they should be open to others only when we wish to give of them. Otherwise they should be and remain our private "business."

29   The desire for privacy is closely linked to the increased insistence on private property in ever-larger aspects of life. My home ought to be the castle where I am protected from anyone's intruding on my privacy. But my home is my castle only when it is my private possession. Understandably, it was the lord of the castle who first claimed privacy for himself and his doings. Thus from the very beginning, demands for privacy were closely connected with private property. Whoever owned no place of his own, owned no privacy either, and he has very little even today. And private property is virtually inseparable from class structure.

30   Only in the seventeenth century, for example, did the common dinner table stop being common to all members of the household, servants and masters alike; no private conversations were held at the dinner table then. In short, the more class-structured a society becomes, the more privacy do its privileged members demand. How understandable, then, that a society which tries to do away with class structure should also try to do away with privacy, and demand that ever larger areas of life should be public.

31   What comes as harder to realize is that as long as everyone knew everything about everyone else there was no need for informers, for elaborate spy systems, or for bugging in order to know what people did, said, and thought. This brings to mind the absence of crime, delinquency, and other asocial behavior in the Israeli kibbutzim. There are no police there, because there is no need for policing. Everyone lives much more collectively and openly with everyone else than among us, and with this, in essence everybody polices everybody else. There is very little privacy and everyone knows just about everything about everyone else. I personally felt suffocated by the lack of privacy, when I lived there for a time. But I could not blind myself to what to me was an astonishing absence of all asocial behavior in this society, as follows from the absence of privacy—or from having everything in the public domain.

32   Servan-Schreiber, in comparing Americans to the French, remarks that "France is a country where distrust of one's neighbor still prevails. This is due to the conviction that men are by nature hostile and egotistical. There-

fore each protects himself from the other through a complex network of laws, which complexity conforms to the French tendency of carefully limiting and defining all aspects of human existence. The straitjacket which results, quite naturally, prevents all change."[3] And it is true that the demand for privacy implies a distrust of others.

33   Where does all this leave me? Despite all of my realizations I do not cherish privacy less, and I still resent deeply any intrusion upon it.

34   I recognize that modern anomy and alienation, even much of modern *tedium vitae*, result from how distantly people live from each other. Most of our social problems, whether distrust by one group in the population of the other—call it racial discrimination, or class hatred—or the prevalence of crime and delinquency, merely reflect this alienation. The best way to do away with them, perhaps the only one, would be to create true communities. But one cannot live in true communality and also keep much of life private to oneself. Many of our laws telling us what to do and what not to do, which even invade our private lives, are intended to make our society more equitable.

35   If consensus does not arise from communal living, from everyone's sharing the same values and having much the same concerns, then it has to be imposed from the outside. But what suffers then is the individualism my own rearing forces me to cherish so highly. So I am caught in my own contradictions, truly a child of our age of transition. At present I see no way to achieve all these good things together: a true community of living, and an individualism safeguarded by privacy. So let me close with some thoughts on the psychological dimensions of the problem.

36   Professionally I am confronted daily with the suffering of emotionally disturbed children who were raised in situations where great privacy deteriorated into complete isolation from others, and with it from themselves. As a result they became desperately fearful and ashamed of any relations with others, or any familiarity with their bodies. It remains for the next generation to see if it can design a model of privacy which is not founded on repression—on feelings of shame about one's body, its function in elimination, its desire for various forms of sexual satisfaction. Maybe the solution is in a much better balance between those areas that should remain private and those we are better off assigning to the public domain. What is certainly needed is a privacy which does not dwarf but enhances our capacity for true intimacy with those who ought to be closest to us.

37   Among the unresolved problems of modern city life today is the prevalence of fear in our streets. I would like to suggest something far removed

---

[3] J. J. Servan-Schreiber, *Le Défi américain* (Paris: Denoel, 1967).

from reconstructing our cities, or an incredible enlarging of the police force and law-enforcing agents within them. What we need, in my opinion, is a return to much smaller, more self-contained communities where a great deal of what is now private can become public; where we would share and know much more about each other, and care about each other, even to the degree of protecting each other's well-being and property. After all, much crime is prevented, and criminals apprehended, when neighbors pay attention and report their observations to the police. In short, what we need is a desire for privacy that is based not on shame or the fear of what others might do to or think of us, but solely on a wish for simple solitude.

38   Maybe what we must strive for is a way of life where we would wish to share far more with each other because we can trust others more than we presently can, but without the community imposing any rules on how one must think, feel, and shape one's life, as was typical before the anonymity of big city life offered protection against such restraints on the individual's chance to find self-realization in his own ways. What would then be kept private would be kept that way not because it was shameful, but because it was valuable. And if there were less emphasis on private property, as in the kibbutz, there would be less need to protect private property, but only private emotions and experiences. If private property were less valued, it would require less protection and would arouse less desire to grab it away on the part of those who do not own it; and then we might come to value the private experience much more highly. Out of the high value we would then place on our own private experience we would come to respect the privacy of others.

39   While the millennium is not about to arrive, there is at least reasonable hope that modern technology will make the necessary types of property so readily available that they will no longer need to be anxiously guarded. Certainly our attitudes toward our bodies and what is shameful about them, needing to be hidden, are changing. We are a long way from accepting the body and its functions freely, but there is hope that the time may come when the desire for privacy will no longer be based on the need to hide what is experienced as the shameful functions of the body. The less we feel ashamed of, the less we feel curiosity about the private life of others. After all, it is the Peeping Tom who knows so little about his own body and emotions, is so afraid and confused about his own sexuality that he is sneakily trying to find out about that of others; it is he who is so embarrassed about his own instinctual desires that he tries to gain satisfaction from embarrassing others.

40   If we all became more secure about our own bodies, more secure economically, socially, and sexually, we would be able to grant others great individual freedom both out of a desire for such freedom for ourselves, and out of a lack of interest in their private lives, because any morbid interest in the other is always the consequence of a felt inadequacy in ourselves. That

is why we are dying to know how others manage things. If we all were able to manage our own lives, we would have little reason to try to manage the lives of others.

41   Neither a medieval absence of privacy, nor a big brother's spying that makes all of our life public, will do. What we must strive for, as so often and in so many other matters, is the right balance between what should be respected and protected as private in our life, and what should be part of our more or less public communal life. Then the home will be just that—neither a castle, nor a public place.

from *"Surviving" and Other Essays* by Bruno Bettelheim. New York: Alfred A. Knopf Inc., 1979.

♦ Understanding Each Other: Discussion Questions

1. How is *privacy* regarded in your culture? Is it as important as it is in other cultures that you know about? Why or why not?

2. How intrusive into personal privacy is the government in your country? How intrusive is the mass media?

3. How do you feel about *muzak*, the piped-in music played on airplanes, in restaurants, in elevators, in doctor's offices, and in other public places? Does it ever get on your nerves?

4. In American culture, judging from this essay, how important are the rights of the individual? The rights of society? In your culture, how important are the rights of the individual? The rights of society?

5. Based on your knowledge of Bruno Bettelheim's background (as detailed briefly in this excerpt), why do you think privacy was so very important to him? In the phrase "an unqualified right," what does the word *unqualified* mean?

6. Do you study or work to music or with the television on?

7. Do people in your culture sit in an unobservable place and watch people go by?

8. Explain the following allusions:

late- and post-Victorian era	the Dutch Masters
paintings of Pieter Breughel	the Beatles
World War II concentration camps	hippies
Michelangelo	Peeping Tom
"big brother"	

9. What does the maxim "A man's house is his castle" mean? Do you have an expression like that in your language?

10. What solution does Bettelheim offer to resolve the problem of the prevalence of fear in contemporary America's city streets?
11. Bettelheim was a well-known child psychiatrist. How is psychoanalysis viewed in your culture? Do people openly seek treatment from psychologists and psychiatrists? What kinds of psychological counseling are available for children?
12. Who was Sigmund Freud? When did he live? What are some of his important contributions to the field of psychiatry and psychoanalysis?

◆ Interactive Grammar and Usage: Rules in Reflection

Confer with a partner and then fill in the blanks with appropriate transitions or conjunctions. Keep in mind that a transition may be an adverb or a key word or phrase which is repeated effectively. Your teacher may give you a list of choices in class. Some of the choices are those found in the reading; others are close in meaning. Your goal is to make a coherent and cohesive passage. Be prepared to explain the reasons for each answer that you select and the pragmatic rules of usage which are implicit here. The first sentence is done for you.

When I studied as a youngster, the door to my room had to be closed; all had to be quiet, <u>and</u> was quiet. _____ 1 _____ 2 could I concentrate on my thoughts _____ 3 my work, to the exclusion of all other distractions. _____ 4 my own children—the generation born during _____ 5 after World War II—studied best with the door open _____ 6 the record player _____ 7 the radio going full blast; in this radically different setting they learned as much _____ 8 as well as I had. Why _____ 9 do I still need a high degree of privacy _____ 10 have to work— _____ 11 at least much prefer to work—only in quiet concentration; _____ 12 _____ 13 do they—like the people in the Breughel painting—need to be in continuous close touch with their age-mates, _____ 14 at least symbolically through a shared musical interest, _____ 15 they want to concentrate on a mentally demanding task?

♦ Increasing Word Power: Vocabulary in Context

Working with a partner, decide on the meaning *in context* of each of the following words or phrases. Then look up each item in a good English-English dictionary. Does the context meaning of the word in the reading differ in any way from the dictionary's definition? If so, how did the context help you understand the meaning of the word as used in the passage?

Word	Meaning in This Context	Dictionary Definition
pervasive		
intrusive		
innocuous		
usurpation		
tacit		
assumption		
totalitarian		
archaic		
public domain		
distract		

Word	Meaning in This Context	Dictionary Definition
immersed		
longings		
vicarious		
alienation		
bespeak		
ambivalence		
therapeutic		
hypocrisy		
broached		
disseminated		
predilections		
deviant		
flaunt		
be ashamed of		
shrink from		
clamor		
neurosis		
circumlocution		
degradation		
bedevil		
skeletons		
affluent		
medieval		
kibbutzim		
egotistical		
anomy		
dwarf		
solitude		
strive for		
millennium		

◆ Finding Your Own Voice: For Discussion and Writing

1. In discussion or debate with your classmates, describe the kind of society in which you would like to be living thirty years from now.
2. Write an essay in which you argue for the establishment of what you would consider to be an ideal society.
3. After discussion or debate with your classmates, write an essay in which you either defend or attack Bettelheim's argument that "a return to much smaller, more self-contained communities where a great deal of what is now private can become public; where we would share and

know much more about each other, and care about each other, even to the degree of protecting each other's well-being and property" would reduce crime and fear on America's city streets.

4. Perform the scenario "Circumstantial evidence" to bring your work with this chapter full circle. Your teacher may ask you to write an essay about the theme of this scenario, by yourself or with other students.

CHAPTER 4

Greek American

♦ Listening to Each Other: Scenario

See Chapter 1 for instructions on how to perform a scenario.
Prepare and perform the scenario "A matter of friendship—and health."

♦ Speaking Out: Debriefing Questions

1. How did the two friends in the scenario resolve their respective dilemmas?
2. Are any other solutions possible?
3. If the scenario were played out again, would you change anything the characters said or did?
4. Do you know of anyone who has had a real experience with this kind of problem? How was it resolved?

♦ Reaching Out: Suggestions for Further Activities

1. In 1990, the restoration of the buildings and grounds of Ellis Island was completed. Ellis Island was the entry point for millions of immigrants to the United States. Prepare a report about Ellis Island and present it in class. Illustrate your talk with pictures of the buildings and grounds on the island.
2. If possible, arrange to visit Ellis Island or a nearby port of entry run by the United States Immigration Service. Gather all the facts you can about how immigrants are processed into the country. Also find out

what the rules and regulations are about bringing animals into the country.

3. Many large American cities have a significant number of Greek Americans. To celebrate their heritage, these people often hold festivals which are open to the public. If possible, go to a Greek festival as a class, and partake of the singing and dancing, the bazaar, and the delicious foods offered. Talk to some Greek Americans and ask them about their culture's contributions to the United States.

4. The reading for this chapter comes from Elia Kazan's book *America America*. If possible, before doing the reading watch *America America*, the movie made from Kazan's book. Make notes on the story, particularly on the ending, where Stavros and his friends arrive by ship in New York City. Then do the reading and compare the handling of the scenes in the book with the way they were handled in the film.

◆ Reading: From *America America*, by Elia Kazan

Read the following selection, keeping in mind the scenario you have already experienced. It is always a good idea to have an English-English dictionary at hand when you read. A useful technique is to read the selection through quickly the first time, highlighting words or phrases you think you need to look up. Then go back and do a more careful reading, looking up unfamiliar words.

This is what happened previously in the story: Stavros was beaten unconscious by ship stewards after he had been provoked into attacking another passenger. His name was turned over to the U.S. Immigration authorities on a charge of criminal assault, which means that he can be arrested and deported if he tries to enter the country.

1   The ship's doctor is a small, worn German, wearing a soiled white jacket. He is soaking a cloth in antiseptic. Now he carries it to where Stavros is lying on a cot in the Ship's Hospital, third class. Hohanness is there. Stavros winces as the doctor applies the cloth.

2   The DOCTOR: "A man shouldn't be hit on the head. It's not as hard as it feels. Let him sleep."

HOHANNESS: "I'll stay with him."

In the middle of the night, Stavros has his first nightmare. Hohanness is on the floor beside him.

Stavros, whispering: "Hohanness!! Hohanness!!"

HOHANNESS: "Yes, yes, I'm here."

STAVROS: "Is my father still here?"

HOHANNESS: "Your what? What? Oh, no, no."

STAVROS: "Isn't that—? Who's that?"

HOHANNESS: "The doctor."

STAVROS: "Is he listening? Can he hear us?"

HOHANNESS: "He's asleep. Don't worry."

Stavros, conspiratorial: "My father said: 'That's enough. I'm ashamed of you. I'm ashamed of what you've made of yourself. Come back, you must start again!'" He bursts out laughing. "It hurts when I laugh. But can you imagine? Making this journey all over again? Allah!!"

HOHANNESS: "Shshsh. That was a dream. Go to sleep."

STAVROS: "Allah! Hohanness, can you imagine?" Again he laughs, again it hurts. "Hohanness, stay with me."

HOHANNESS: "I'll be here when you wake."

Stavros is almost asleep now. His face darkens, he looks troubled.

STAVROS: "You know the truth? The thing I'd like most in the world is to start this journey over. That's the truth! Just to start it over, all over again . . . oh . . . oh . . ."

Hohanness is very moved. Suddenly he has a terrible fit of coughing. His eyes swing around to the doctor, who is awakened by Hohanness' cough.

DOCTOR: "How is he?"

Hohanness, frightened: "He's imagining things."

DOCTOR: "Well, no wonder! He was hit on the head once too often. You better watch over him. Stay close to him."

HOHANNESS: "I will."

DOCTOR: "He's liable to do something crazy. Goodnight. That's a bad cough you've got yourself. Better not let the Americans hear that tomorrow. They'll send you back."

3   On the front deck the next day, one sees very little for the fog. *The Kaiser Wilhelm* is moving slowly forward. The usual harbor noises. Out of the fog, as if coming toward the ship, is the Statue of Liberty. As they see it, the passengers stand. There is a sound—is it imagined?—of a general sigh.

4   A large motor launch is coming alongside. Officials of the United States Health Service prepare to board ship.

5   Stavros wears a bandage. There is about him the manic desperation of the suicide-to-be.

6   One of the shoeshine boys has been sent to fetch Hohanness. He calls him, waves, calls again . . .

7   Hohanness starts off. Stavros pulls him back and, in whispers, gives him his final instructions.

8   STAVROS: "It's the excitement that brings on your cough. So, close your ears. Imagine you've just put down your well. And your mother and father come to you in gratitude. Can you imagine that scene?"

HOHANNESS: "Oh, yes, yes!"

STAVROS: "I'll wait for you just down the corridor. The instant the inspection is over, run to me."

He indicates to Hohanness he can go, pushes him off, but the boy comes back.

HOHANNESS: "But you, what are you going to do?"

STAVROS: "I have my own plans."

Hohanness comes close, whispers.

HOHANNESS: "What?"

Stavros makes a subtle proud little gesture which says, "Over the side and swim for it."

HOHANNESS: "Can you swim that far?"

Stavros turns his face away: "They say a man learns what is necessary to save his life."

HOHANNESS: "Stavros, if you can't swim, you can't swim."

STAVROS: "You better go. Go on, go on."

HOHANNESS: "And if you go down?"

STAVROS: "Better than going back." He pushes him off. "Go on! They're waiting."

Hohanness seizes Stavros' hand and kisses it.

HOHANNESS: "I'll pay you back, some day. I'll pay you back . . ."

Stavros, tough: "Let's speak the truth. We'll never see each other after tomorrow. You'll forget me. And I? I'll be where I am."

9   The shoeshine boys are all gathered in their little cabin, sitting on the edge of their bunks. Mr. Agnostis and the Public Health official are in the middle of the floor.

10   MR. AGNOSTIS: "Same as last year. Eight fine boys."

Hohanness is following Stavros' instructions. One side of his head is pressed hard into the pillow. A hand covers the other ear. He is imagining the scene at the well and his parents' gratitude.

MR. AGNOSTIS: "All from fine families. Perfect health. Employment guaranteed. Nothing to worry. Everything under control!"

At the end of the corridor, Stavros waits.

Hohanness' eyes shine with his imaginings.

HEALTH OFFICIAL: "OK, OK."

11   He comes out of the shoeshine boys' cabin and heads in the direction of Stavros, behind him the first buzz of celebration.

12   Stavros waits for the official to pass him. Behind him sounds of the boys celebrating are heard. Then suddenly we hear, dominating all other sounds, Hohanness' terrible cough. Stavros hears this, and suddenly he has an impulse to stop and delay the official so that he too will hear the cough. Then, just as the official gets real close, Stavros turns and faces the side wall of the corridor. He has controlled his impulse to betray his friend. He now flattens his face against the wall. The health official passes by Stavros, entering the doorway behind.

13   Stavros, face to wall, still shakes from the excitement of what he almost did. Hohanness, wildly elated, runs out of the cabin and comes towards Stavros, hysterical with delight and relief.

14   Hohanness: "Stavros! Stavros!"

15   Then he begins to cough, this time beyond control. At the moment he gets to Stavros, his cough overwhelms him. He falls into the arms of his friend, in total collapse.

16   The door into which the health official disappeared was that of the Ship's Hospital, third class. Now attracted by the terrible coughing, the health official comes to the doorway. Behind him appears the Ship's Doctor. There is no longer any doubt as to what Hohanness' fate will be.

17   Stavros holds Hohanness. He looks at the official.

18   In the shoeshine boys' cabin, a conference is going on. All are present. Mr. Agnostis is talking to Stavros.

19   MR. AGNOSTIS: "I tell you *I* take you. But read! Here! U.S. Government paper. Where is your name here? Where? You want me in jail?"

Silence. They all sit in silence.

HOHANNESS: "Take my name. I beg you. Take Hohanness Gardashian."

MR. AGNOSTIS: "There can't be two of you!! There can't be two Hohanness Gardashians. Give up. Go back together. Keep each other company."

20   That night celebrations break out all over the ship. Disembarkation is at seven the next morning. It is the last night for the shipboard friendships.

21   At the prow, Stavros and Hohanness huddle together, their arms around each other's shoulders.

22   HOHANNESS: "When?"

STAVROS: "As soon as everyone's asleep."

HOHANNESS: "I won't let you . . ."

Stavros turns and smiles at Hohanness, a smile superior and determined, half scorn, half affection, unswayable.

A swirl of First Class passengers rush to the prow of the ship. The women are in long light-colored dresses.

A GIRL: "Oh, Third Class is so romantic!"

MAN: "They've got the best part of the ship."

HOHANNESS: "I mean it. If you go, I go to . . . And I can't swim. I'll hold on to you. I'll call out. I won't let you go. I won't!" He pleads with his friend. "Stavros, please, please don't be crazy. Don't be."

23   He is weeping.

24   The celebrants have brought musicians with them who now strike up. The First Class begins to waltz.

25   Stavros is full of envy, anger, and revenge. He leaps up and into the middle of the dancers, doing weird, manic leaps and turns.

26   Man: "Say, look out there. Look out!"

27   Stavros leaps and kicks out into the air like an insane man. Savage, uncontrollable cries escape his mouth. All the pain that's been stored up in him for months and months!

28   Hohanness watches Stavros with absolute love. Now Stavros begins to whirl like the dervishes of Konya, around and around, head tilted on one

side, his eyes shining with a fanatical light. Hohanness, never taking his eyes off Stavros, rises slowly. Stavros dances wilder and wilder. More and more desperate! Hohanness turns abruptly and looks over the rail. A sudden impulse. He sees the black water of the bay. Each time this boy has said, "Before it eats me!" he has gently touched his chest with the palm of his right hand. Now he makes this gesture for the last time.

29   Stavros has won the admiration of the celebrants. They cheer.

30   Unseen, Hohanness goes over the rail and lets himself drop into the black waters of the bay.

31   The First Class passengers applaud and cheer Stavros. The moment they do this, he stops. He doesn't want anything from them, not even their admiration. He looks them over with fantastic hostility. Then spits out his "Allah!" and struts off.

32   Terror overcomes Hohanness in the water. He begins to cough. He goes down, comes up, coughing, his strength ebbing fast. He goes down.

33   The celebrants follow Stavros, begging him to dance some more, the girls beguiling, flirting with this wild boy, not letting him go.

34   In the black waters of the bay there is no longer any sign of Hohanness.

35   Stavros pushes off the celebrants, walks up to where he left Hohanness. He looks around for him, calls softly: "Hohanness, Hohanness!" Softly, gently, "Hohanness."

36   The First Class is disembarking. A band plays a gay exit march. The Third Class watches. Their turn will come later.

37   The eight shoeshine boys, now with Stavros instead of Hohanness, are looking up at the passengers of the First Class leaving the ship. Sophia and Aratoon disembark from the gangplank. Neither looks back. Stavros expected no goodbye. A tap on his shoulder.

38   It is Bertha, in a hurry. She extends a paper bag and an envelope.

39   Bertha: "Here! From Mrs. Kebabian."

40   She turns and goes. Stavros takes out of the paper sack a man's straw hat. He looks at it, smiles, puts it on. Under his breath he says, "Allah!" Then he opens the envelope. It contains a piece of paper money. Nothing else. Mr. Agnostis and the boys gather around.

41   Mr. Agnostis: "Ooohhh! Fifty dollars! OOOOHHHH!!!!"

42   In the immigration shed on Ellis Island, three long lines of people lead to three desks. At one of the desks, the eight shoeshine boys, led by Mr. Agnostis, come up for their turn. Stavros is wearing his straw hat. Mr. Agnostis has papers in hand and now presents them to the Immigration official at this desk. The official has seen Agnostis before.

43   OFFICIAL: "Oh, look who's here! And eight more little ones! They keep coming, they keep coming! How are all your little slaves?"

Mr. Agnostis' laugh is a nervous one. The boys stare anxiously.

OFFICIAL: "Scared to death." He turns to the official at the next desk. "Jack! Who was that fellow—a Greek—we're watching for? Criminal assault was it?"

Stavros watches intently. Mr. Agnostis bends over, pretending to tie his shoelace. He has palmed a ten dollar bill and is preparing to slide it towards the shoe of the official, who raises it ever so slightly off the floor. Meantime . . .

JACK: "On the yellow sheet—that's it."

Stavros is watching the ten dollar bill and the foot of the official.

STAVROS: "Allah!"

It's not much of a sound. It's rather a kind of growl. But it does voice protest. His dream is being shattered.

The official looks at Stavros. Then he smiles in a peculiarly combative manner. He picks up the yellow sheet.

Official, mispronouncing it of course: "Stavros Topouzoglou. Any of you go by that name?"

MR. AGNOSTIS: "That fellow died last night."

OFFICIAL: "You? What's your name?"

He is looking at Stavros again.

MR. AGNOSTIS: "Hohanness."

OFFICIAL: "Not you, *you!* He talks doesn't he? What's your name?"

Stavros now has the idea: "Hohanness Gardashian."

OFFICIAL: "You want to be an American?"

MR. AGNOSTIS: "Oh yes, sir. Yes, sir."

OFFICIAL: "Well, the first thing to do is change that name? You want an American name, boy?"

Mr. Agnostis is indicating to Stavros to agree, but Stavros doesn't quite understand.

Stavros, vehemently: "Hohanness Gardashian."

OFFICIAL: "I know, I know."

Stavros, almost a shout: "Hohanness!"

Official, quickly: "That's enough! Hohanness. That's all you need here."

He writes something on a piece of paper and hands it to Stavros.

OFFICIAL: "Here! Can you read?"

Stavros, of course, cannot. Mr. Agnostis comes up and reads: "Joe Arness." Then he gets it. "Hohanness. Joe Arness. Hohanness." He turns to Stavros. "Joe Arness. Joe."

Stavros, repeating: "Joe."

MR. AGNOSTIS: "Arness."

STAVROS: "Arness."

Mr. Agnostis, points to him: "Joe Arness."

Stavros, nodding acknowledgment: "Joe Arness."

Mr. Agnostis, to official: "Good!"

Stavros, to official: "Joe Arness."

Official, full of the pride of authorship: "You like it?"

Stavros nods, makes signs, etc.: "Joe Arness, Joe Arness, good, good!"

OFFICIAL: "Well boy, you're reborn. You're baptized again. And without benefit of clergy. Next!"

Mr. Agnostis and the eight boys leave for the ferryboat to Manhattan. The Ellis Island immigration shed is empty now except for the three officials. They are looking at one object: Stavros' hamal's harness.

SECOND OFFICIAL: "What the hell is that?"

OFFICIAL: "Oh, something one of them left behind."

44 On the ferry.

45 STAVROS: "So . . . it's the same here!? He took money!"

MR. AGNOSTIS: "People take money everywhere. But did you see him jump when you spoke? Did you see him jump?"

STAVROS: "Yes. Allah!"

46 Mr. Agnostis laughs. And now Stavros joins in, the first full, simple, free laugh heard from the boy since he left home. Now the others join in, all laughing.

47 Down the last gangplank come the eight boys and Mr. Agnostis. Stavros first. He falls on his knees and kisses the ground! Then he lifts up and releases a tremendous shout of joy.

from Kazan, Elia. *America, America,* 1961, 1962. Originally published by Stein & Day, Inc., reprinted with permission of Scarborough House/Publishers.

♦ Understanding Each Other: Discussion Questions

1. Have you or has anyone you know become seriously ill or been hospitalized while in the United States? Did you notice any differences from your native culture in the way that American doctors and nurses perform their duties and in the way that American hospitals are run? What rules must hospital visitors follow in the United States? In your country?

2. What is a *shoeshine boy?* Do you have the equivalent in your culture?

3. Who are the dervishes of Konya?

4. What is the relationship between Stavros and Hohanness like? Describe it in detail, using evidence from the story to support your answer.

5. What happens to Hohanness? What kind of a sacrifice does he make for Stavros? Does Stavros encourage him to do it in any way?

6. How does Stavros get the name "Joe Arness"?

7. How old would you guess Stavros and Hohanness are?

8. What kind of a person is the immigration official who interviews Mr. Agnostis and Stavros? List at least five adjectives to describe him.

9. How were you treated when you came through the United States Customs and Immigration Service? Do you have any suggestions to make for improving the process?

10. What is Mr. Agnostis's role in the story? Did Mr. Agnostis come on the ship with Stavros and Hohanness, or was he already in the United States? What clues from the story can you cite to support your answer?

11. A *symbol* is an object which represents, or stands for, something else. For example, a *flag* symbolizes the country it represents. There are several symbols in this story. The Statue of Liberty and the hamal's harness are two of the most important ones. Read an article about the Statue of Liberty. What does it represent to Americans? To immigrants? Look up the word *hamal* in a good English-English dictionary. What is it? What does it symbolize (represent) to Stavros? What other symbols can you find in the story?

◆ Interactive Grammar and Usage: Rules in Reflection

Kazan uses adverbs and prepositional phrases in the function of adverbs to create vivid imagery. Work with another student and fill in the blanks with appropriate adverbs to complete the following passage. Your teacher may give you a list of words to choose from. You will notice that some of the choices are those found in the reading; others are close in meaning. Be prepared to explain the reasons for your choices. Then state the rules governing the placement of adverbs in English sentences. Have your choices affected the *tone* of the passage? In what ways? The first sentence is done for you.

Hohanness watches Stavros <u>with absolute love</u>. <u>Now</u> Stavros begins to whirl like the dervishes of Konya, <u>around</u> and <u>around</u>, head titled <u>on one side</u>, his eyes shining <u>with a fanatical light</u>. Hohanness, _____ 1 taking his eyes _____ 2 , rises _____ 3 . Stavros dances _____ 4 and _____ 4 . _____ 5 and _____ 5 desperate! Hohanness turns _____ 6 and looks _____ 7 . A sudden impulse. He sees the black water of the bay. Each time this boy has said," _____ 8 it eats me!" he has _____ 9 touched his chest _____ 10 of his right hand. _____ 11 he makes this gesture for the last time. . . .

_____ 12 , Hohanness goes _____ 13 and lets himself drop _____ 14 of the bay.

♦ Increasing Word Power: Vocabulary in Context

Working with a partner, decide on the meaning *in context* of each of the following words or phrases. Then look up each item in a good English-English dictionary. Does the context meaning of the word in the reading differ in any way from the dictionary's definition? If so, how did the context help you understand the meaning of the word as used in the passage?

Word	Meaning in This Context	Dictionary Definition
soaking		
antiseptic		
wince		
nightmare		
conspiratorial		
be moved		
liable		
launch		
manic		
corridor		
subtle		
bunks		
buzz		
impulse		
betray		
elated		

Word	Meaning in This Context	Dictionary Definition
disembarkation		
the prow		
huddle		
unswayable		
swirl		
waltz		
revenge		
weird		
fanatical		
abruptly		
ebbing		
beguiling		
flirting		
intently		
palm		
growl		
voice		
shattered		
peculiarly		
combative		
vehemently		
nodding		
baptized		
without benefit of clergy		

◆ Finding Your Own Voice: For Discussion and Writing

1. With which character in the story did you identify? Explain why you liked that character. Did you *dislike* any character in the story? Which one, and why?

2. What were your first feelings and impressions when you arrived in the United States? Discuss them with your classmates and then describe them as vividly as you can. Use adjectives, adverbs, and active-voice verbs to capture those images. Write a story or essay.

3. Compare your first impressions of the United States with the impressions you have now, after being in the country for some time. Be as specific as you can in describing how they are different.

4. Perform the scenario "Love or expediency" to bring your work with this chapter full circle. Your teacher may ask you to write an essay about the theme of this scenario, by yourself or with other students.

CHAPTER 5

Hispanic American

◆ Listening to Each Other: Scenario

See Chapter 1 for instructions on how to perform a scenario.

Prepare and perform the scenario "What price companionship?" If there is time, perform "Dating American style."

◆ Speaking Out: Debriefing Questions

1. How did each participant in the scenario react to the new country and to the new school?
2. If you were in the same situation in real life, would you come up with the same solutions they did?
3. Can you identify all the problems that each character had? Who had the major problems? The minor problems? Who had solutions? What were they?
4. If you could play a role other than the one you were assigned (either as a direct participant or as a member of the support group), which one would you choose?
5. Would you change anything if the scenario were acted out a second time?

◆ Reaching Out: Suggestions for Further Activities

1. Have you ever experienced a situation like the one in this scenario? Do you know anyone who has? How was the situation resolved? Describe the experience to the class.
2. Replay the scenario with this new information: (1) the grandparents are relatively young; (2) the mother has an American suitor.
3. Extrapolate any axioms or proverbs you can from the scenario. Divide the class into small groups. Each team must present a different axiom, without identifying the moral. The rest of the class should listen carefully and guess the axiom or proverb.
4. If possible, watch the film *Stand and Deliver*. Take notes on how the characters in the film live and think, and on how they handle their problems, so that you can compare the movie with the reading.
5. Write an essay about the theme of the scenario and bring it into class for the group to critique and polish.

◆ Reading: From *Barrio Boy*, by Ernesto Galarza

Read the following selection, keeping in mind the scenario you have already experienced. It is always a good idea to have an English-English dictionary at hand when you read. A useful technique is to read the selection through quickly the first time, highlighting words or phrases that you think you need to look up. Then go back and do a more careful reading, looking up unfamiliar words.

1   The lower quarter was not exclusively a Mexican *barrio* but a mix of many nationalities. Between L and N Streets two blocks from us, the Japanese had taken over. Their homes were in the alleys behind shops, which they advertised with signs covered with black scribbles. The women walked on the street in kimonos, wooden sandals, and white stockings, carrying neat black bundles on their backs and wearing their hair in puffs with long ivory needles stuck through them. When they met they bowed, walked a couple of steps, and turned and bowed again, repeating this several times. They carried babies on their backs, not in their arms, never laughed or went into the saloons. On Sundays the men sat in front of their shops, dressed in gowns, like priests.

2   Chinatown was on the other side of K Street, toward the Southern Pacific shops. Our houses were old, but those in which the Chinese kept stores, laundries, and restaurants were older still. In black jackets and skullcaps the older merchants smoked long pipes with a tiny brass cup on the end. In their dusty store windows there was always the same assortment of

tea packages, rice bowls, saucers, and pots decorated with blue temples and dragons.

3   In the hotels and rooming houses scattered about the *barrio* the Filipino farm workers, riverboat stewards, and houseboys made their homes. Like the Mexicans they had their own poolhalls, which they called clubs. Hindus from the rice and fruit country north of the city stayed in the rooming houses when they were in town, keeping to themselves. The Portuguese and Italian families gathered in their own neighborhoods along Fourth and Fifth Streets southward toward the Y-street levee. The Poles, Yugo-Slavs, and Koreans, too few to take over any particular part of it, were scattered throughout the *barrio*. Black men drifted in and out of town, working the waterfront. It was a kaleidoscope of colors and languages and customs that surprised and absorbed me at every turn. . . .

4   We in the *barrio* considered that there were two kinds of *trabajo*. There were the seasonal jobs, some of them a hundred miles or more from Sacramento. And there were the closer *chanzas* to which you could walk or ride on a bicycle. These were the best ones, in the railway shops, the canneries, the waterfront warehouses, the lumber yards, the produce markets, the brick kilns, and the rice mills. To be able to move from the seasonal jobs to the close-in work was a step up the ladder. Men who had made it passed the word along to their relatives or their friends when there was a *chanza* of this kind.

5   It was all done by word of mouth, this delicate wiring of the grapevine. The exchange points of the network were the places where men gathered in small groups, apparently to loaf and chat to no purpose. One of these points was our kitchen, where my uncles and their friends sat and talked of *el macizo* and of the revolution but above all of the *chanzas* they had heard of.

6   There was not only the everlasting talk about *trabajo*, but also the never-ending action of the *barrio* itself. If work was action the *barrio* was where the action was. Every morning a parade of men in oily work clothes and carrying lunch buckets went up Fourth Street toward the railroad shops, and every evening they walked back, grimy and silent. Horse drawn drays with low platforms rumbled up and down our street carrying the goods the city traded in, from kegs of beer to sacks of grain. Within a few blocks of our house there were smithies, hand laundries, a macaroni factory, and all manner of places where wagons and buggies were repaired, horses stabled, bicycles fixed, chickens dressed, clothes washed and ironed, furniture repaired, candy mixed, tents sewed, wine grapes pressed, bottles washed, lumber sawed, suits fitted and tailored, watches and clocks taken apart and put together again, vegetables sorted, railroad cars unloaded, boxcars iced, barges freighted, ice cream cones molded, soda pop bottled, fish scaled, salami stuffed, corn ground for masa, and bread ovened. To those who knew where these were located in the alleys, as I did, the whole *barrio* was an open workshop. The people who worked there came to know you, let you look in at the door, made jokes, and occasionally gave you an odd job.

7   This was the business district of the *barrio*. Around it and through it moved a constant traffic of drays, carts, bicycles, pushcarts, trucks, and high-wheeled automobiles with black canvas tops and honking horns. On the tailgates of drays and wagons, I nipped rides when I was going home with a gunnysack full of empty beer bottles or my gleanings around the packing sheds. . . .

8   Like the first grade, the rest of the Lincoln School was a sampling of the lower part of town where many races made their home. My pals in the second grade were Kazushi, whose parents spoke only Japanese; Matti, a skinny Italian boy; and Manuel, a fat Portuguese who would never get into a fight but wrestled you to the ground and just sat on you. Our assortment of nationalities included Koreans, Yugoslavs, Poles, Irish, and home-grown Americans.

9   Miss Hopley and her teachers never let us forget why we were at Lincoln: for those who were alien, to become good Americans; for those who were so born, to accept the rest of us. Off the school grounds we traded the same insults we heard from our elders. On the playground we were sure to be marched up to the principal's office for calling someone a wop, a chink, a dago, or a greaser. The school was not so much a melting pot as a griddle where Miss Hopley and her helpers warmed knowledge into us and roasted racial hatreds out of us.

10   At Lincoln, making us into Americans did not mean scrubbing away what made us originally foreign. The teachers called us as our parents did, or as close as they could pronounce our names in Spanish or Japanese. No one was ever scolded or punished for speaking in his native tongue on the playground. Matti told the class about his mother's down quilt, which she had made in Italy with the fine feathers of a thousand geese. Encarnación acted out how boys learned to fish in the Phillipines. I astounded the third grade with the story of my travels on a stagecoach, which nobody else in the class had seen except in the museum at Sutter's Fort. After a visit to the Crocker Art Gallery and its collection of heroic paintings of the golden age of California, someone showed a silk scroll with a Chinese painting. Miss Hopley herself had a way of expressing wonder over these matters before a class, her eyes wide open until they popped slightly. It was easy for me to feel that becoming a proud American, as she said we should, did not mean feeling ashamed of being a Mexican.

11   The Americanization of Mexican me was no smooth matter. I had to fight one lout who made fun of my travels on the *diligencia,* and my barbaric translation of the word into "diligence." He doubled up with laughter over the word until I straightened him out with a kick. In class I made points explaining that in Mexico roosters said "qui-qui-ri-qui" and not "cock-a-doodle-doo," but after school I had to put up with the taunts of a big Yugoslav who said Mexican roosters were crazy. . . .

12   I came back to the Lincoln School after every summer, moving up through the grades with Miss Campbell, Miss Beakey, Mrs. Wood, Miss

Applegate, and Miss Delahunty. I sat in the classroom adjoining the principal's office and had my turn answering her telephone when she was about the building repeating the message to the teacher, who made a note of it. Miss Campbell read to us during the last period of the week about King Arthur, Columbus, Buffalo Bill, and Daniel Boone, who came to life in the reverie of the class through the magic of her voice. And it was Miss Campbell who introduced me to the public library on Eye Street, where I became a regular customer.

13   All of Lincoln School mourned together when Eddie, the blond boy everybody liked, was killed by a freight train as he crawled across the tracks going home one day. We assembled to say good-bye to Miss Applegate, who was off to Alaska to be married. Now it was my turn to be excused from class to interpret for a parent enrolling a new student fresh from Mexico. Graduates from Lincoln came back now and then to tell us about high school. A naturalist entertained us in assembly, imitating the calls of the meadow lark, the water ouzel, the oriole, and the killdeer. I decided to become a bird man after I left Lincoln. . . .

14   The *barrio*, without particularly planning it that way, was providing me with an education out of school as well as in. I did not think of 418 L Street and the Lincoln School as in any way alike, but both had a principal, Miss Hopley and Mrs. Dodson. From Miss Hopley I learned that the man with the black beard and the sad eyes pictured on her wall was Abraham Lincoln, for whom our school was named. From Mrs. Dodson I found out that the picture of the nude lady was September Morn and that it was a famous painting. Miss Hopley conducted me firmly and methodically through the grades into the new world of books and manners she called America. Mrs. Dodson adopted us into the odd company of the rooming house, from which I found my way through the *barrio*.

15   When the Sumo wrestlers from Japan put on a match in a tent raised on a vacant lot, somebody in the house got me a job giving out handbills and a pass for my work. Wedged in a Japanese audience I saw two mountains of fat dressed in loincloths trying to kill each other. At 418 L with the help of my neighbors, I lined up business for a traveling photographer who took pictures of children sitting on a donkey that reminded me, joyfully, of our Relámpago in Jalcocotán. Mr. Hans gave us front porch lectures on the electric automobiles that passed by—stiff black boxes gliding by without a sound and without a smell with stiff ladies at the steering bar, also in black. There was an arrangement with the bartender on Fourth Street by which I could buy a pail of draught beer by signaling him from the alley door marked "Family Entrance." The cop on the beat objected mildly to this, as he did to Cho-ree's allowing me to nip rides on his truck. To please him we did it only when he was somewhere else in the *barrio*.

16   Once in a while, I also managed to get around the rule that I was not to run to skid row whenever a street fight was on. These fights were regular, especially on Saturday nights, and the news of a brawl spread fast. If they

happened when I was on the waterfront my attendance at these bloody events was no problem. I simply joined the crowd. In one of these fights I saw Speedy and another American battle with their fists, both men streaming blood from their faces. The fight between two Mexicans was something memorable. I arrived in time to see the police loading the winner into the paddy wagon, and the loser lying in the alley in a bloody shirt. And there was the fire in our alley that burned down a shack and cremated an old man who lived there. A house was blown up on T Street, by the Black Hand, it was said. I walked by the place with Catfish stealthily. We thought we could see the smudged imprint of the Hand on the blasted chimney.

17   When there was a fight, a fire, or a murder the government paid a great deal of attention to the *barrio*. Police and firemen swarmed around for a while. We never called the police, they just came. José explained the wisdom of this to me. "When *los chotas* start asking questions," he said, "you never know what they will ask next." About one thing the entire *barrio* seemed to be in agreement: the dirtiest, most low-down human being was the stool pigeon, the sneak who turned you in to the Authorities.

18   Most of the time things were quiet in the lower part of town. The cop on our beat, with the half-moon palms and a double row of brass buttons on his uniform, walked by running his billy club along the pickets of our front fence and nodding at the porch sitters as he passed. The others, the ones that cruised in the paddy wagon, were less friendly.

19   The boys in our section of the *barrio* sorted themselves out by age, game skills of various kinds, and common causes against families, policemen, and other hazards. Russell, Sammie, Catfish, and I organized something that was neither a club nor a gang but could become either. Two people gave us a purpose for organizing—the floor walker of the basement store of Weinstock's, which faced our house; and Van, a *barrio* drifter who was much interested in younger boys.

20   The floor walker was a giant of a man who guarded the toys that Weinstock's displayed and which we had no money to buy. The vigilante seemed to be everywhere, towering over the aisles of the store whenever we were wandering about, usually in pairs. In spite of him, Russell and Catfish had managed to lift a toy pistol and parts of an Erector set which they couldn't take home—for obvious reasons.

21   By a piece of luck Russell and I discovered a loose plank that hung by a single nail on the fence next to the Chinese laundry in the alley. The plank swung on the nail enough to allow us to squeeze through. Behind it there was a narrow passage enclosed on three sides by fencing, a no-man's-land that had been forgotten when the fences were built. There was room for five or six of us squatting, and no houses close enough for people to hear us if we talked in low voices.

22   The forgotten nook became our clubhouse which soon had a professional manager, Van himself.

23   He was twice our age and impressed us with a swagger we vaguely admired. He said he had been in the reform school in a place called Pájaro Valley, had fooled the cops many times, and thought that floor walkers were stupid if you knew how to operate. Besides, he could teach us to smoke Fatimas and Cubebs.

24   Even though all the club members could not get together at one time because of family interference, Van was always there to push our education. He brought cigarettes and passed the butts around. He demonstrated how we would get over the sour taste and the coughing once we learned to inhale. Van always carried a packet of pictures of naked ladies to show us. When he got back to the matter of Weinstock's he guaranteed that he could work out a plan to sneak a whole Erector set, box and all, in one swoop—if we listened to him.

25   Sammie, the nephew of the Jewish shoemaker up L Street; Catfish, the Japanese toughie; Russell the gringo, and I were plainly getting inside information on the lower part of town from Van. He knew a man who would buy copper wire, tools or anything else we could pilfer, all of which could be kept safely among the weeds of our hideout.

26   All this presented problems about what not to tell our families and Van swore us to secrecy.

27   Ours turned out to be the *barrio* club with the shortest history of any similar establishment in the United States. The loose plank which was our entrance to the underworld was in plain view of everyone who lived in the alley. Besides, we made a fatal mistake. I nominated Albert, Lettie's young son, for membership, and to try him out I showed him our quarters one afternoon when his mother was not at home. We never found out whether it was Albert or the Chinese laundryman next door to our club or Stacey who turned us in, but soon after Albert's initiation it happened. Van was giving Catfish, Sammie, and me an illustrated lecture which had something to do with the naked ladies of his pictures, when the plank moved, wrenched loose by Doña Henriqueta and Lettie. Since there was no emergency exit to our clubhouse there was nothing for Van to do but to shut up, for Catfish to drop the butt, and for me to look as if I didn't understand English and knew nothing of what was going on. I was confined to my own back yard on Saturdays and Sundays. Sammie's uncle made him punch leather every day after school and watch the shop when he should have been playing with us. Catfish got a beating. Van disappeared.

28   It was not likely that I would have made as much pilfering at Weinstock's or selling stolen property as I did at my odd jobs. On the other hand, as Van had explained, you could learn to stick up a bank and live the rest of your life a rich man.

29   Whatever the case, when the raid blasted my chances of a successful gang career, the Lincoln School, 418 L and the *barrio* kept me busy enough, and straight.

30   Luckily, also, even though my gang was broken up, my friendships were not. Catfish and I continued to explore the waterfront together, bringing home our catch from the river and the pick-ups from the produce markets to show that we had been absent on legitimate business. My gang-busting mother became fond of Sammie, who was invited to supper occasionally and once to spend the night with us, sharing my bathroom bunk. We conversed in pig Latin, at which he was an expert, and translated questions I asked him into Hebrew in exchange for questions he asked me which I translated into Spanish. What I told him about Mexicans struck him as odd or comical, but no more so than I thought some of the things he told me about Jews. Sammie could have been adopted at 418 L Street by way of our family, but one day his uncle was beaten up. He died, the shop was closed, and I never saw Sammie again. . . .

31   At about this time my mother remarried. We made room for my stepfather, a *chicano* who had come to California not too long after us. His problems with the Americans were the same as ours, especially their language.

32   To begin with, we didn't hear one but many sorts of English. Mr. Chester, my soldier friend, and Big Ernie spoke as if they were tired and always arguing. The Old Gentleman nibbled his words, like a rabbit working on a carrot, perhaps because all his teeth weren't there. Mr. Brien's words came through in a deep voice from behind the hair screen of his moustache. Big Singh spoke English in his own way, brittle and choppy, hard to understand unless you watched his lips. These people sounded nothing like the Sicilian vegetable hawker or the Greek grocer at the corner or the black lady in the alley who saved beer bottles for me. And of course none of them sounded like Miss Hopley or Miss Campbell.

33   It took time to realize that when the Americans said "Sackmenna" they meant Sacra-men-to, or that "Kelly-phony" was their way of saying Cali-for-nia. Worse yet, the names of many of their towns could not be managed. I tried to teach Gustavo that Woodland was not pronounced "Boor-lan," and that Walnut Grove was not "Gualen-gro." A secondhand shop on our block that called itself The Cheap Store sounded to us like the Sheep Store, and the sign did not spell it like the school books.

34   There was no authority at 418 L who could tell us the one proper way to pronounce a word and it would not have done much good if there had been. Try as they did the adults in my family could see no difference between "wood" and "boor." Words spelled the same way or nearly so in Spanish and English and whose meanings we could guess accurately— words like *principal* and *tomato*—were too few to help us in daily usage. The grown-ups adapted the most necessary words and managed to make themselves understood, words like the *French loff, yelly-rol, eppel pai, teekett,* and *kenn meelk.* Miss Campbell and her colleagues lost no time in scrubbing out these spots in my own pronunciation. Partly to show off, partly to do my duty to the family, I tried their methods at home. It was

hopeless. They listened hard but they couldn't hear me. Besides, *Boor-lan* was *Boor-lan* all over the *barrio*. Everyone knew what you meant even though you didn't say Woodland. I gave up giving English lessons at home.

35   The *barrio* invented its own versions of American talk. And my family, to my disgust, adopted them with no little delight. My mother could tell someone at the door asking for an absent one: "Ess gon." When some American tried to rush her into conversation she stopped him with: "Yo no pick een-glees." But at *pocho* talk my mother drew the line, although José and Gustavo fell into it easily. Such words as *yarda* for yard, *yonque* for junk, *donas* for doughnuts, *grocería* for grocery store, *raite* for ride, and *borde* for meals shocked her and I was drilled to avoid them. Woolworth's was *el fei-en-ten* to the *barrio* but it was *el baratillo* to her and by command to me also. Gustavo could say *droguería* because there wasn't anything she could do about it, but for me *botica* was required.

36   Prowling the alleys and gleaning along the waterfront I learned how *chicano* workingmen hammered the English language to their ways. On the docks I heard them bark over a slip or a spill: "Oh, Chet," imitating the American crew bosses with the familiar "Gar-demme-yoo." José and I privately compared notes in the matter of "San Afabeechee," who, he said, was a saint of the Americans but which, as I well knew, was what Americans called each other in a fist fight.

37   Our family conversations always occurred on our own kitchen porch, away from the gringos. One or the other of the adults would begin: *Se han fijado?* Had we noticed—that the Americans do not ask permission to leave the room; that they had no respectful way of addressing an elderly person; that they spit brown over the railing of the porch into the yard; that when they laughed they roared; that they never brought *saludos* to everyone in your family from everyone in their family when they visited; that *General Delibree* was only a clerk; that *zopilotes* were not allowed on the streets to collect garbage; that the policemen did not carry lanterns at night; that Americans didn't keep their feet on the floor when they were sitting; that there was a special automobile for going to jail; that a rancho was not a rancho at all but a very small hacienda; that the saloons served their customers free eggs, pickles, and sandwiches; that instead of bullfighting, the gringos for sport tried to kill each other with gloves?

38   I did not have nearly the strong feelings on these matters that Doña Henriqueta expressed. I felt a vague admiration for the way Mr. Brien could spit brown. Wayne, my classmate, laughed much better than the Mexicans, because he opened his big mouth wide and brayed like a donkey so he could be heard a block away. But it was the kind of laughter that made my mother tremble, and it was not permitted in our house.

39   Rules were laid down to keep me, as far as possible, *un muchacho bien educado*. If I had to spit I was to do it privately, or if in public, by the curb, with my head down and my back to people. I was never to wear my cap in the house and I was to take it off even on the porch if ladies or elderly gen-

tlemen were sitting. If I wanted to scratch, under no circumstances was I to do it right then and there, in company, like the Americans, but I was to excuse myself. If Catfish or Russell yelled to me from across the street I was not to shout back. I was never to ask for tips for my errands or other services to the tenants of 418 L, for these were *atenciones* expected of me.

40   Above all I was never to fail in *respeto* to grownups, no matter who they were. It was an inflexible rule; I addressed myself to *Señor* Big Singh, *Señor* Big Ernie, *Señora* Dodson, *Señor* Cho-ree Lopez.

41   My standing in the family, but especially with my mother depended on my keeping these rules. I was not punished for breaking them. She simply reminded me that it gave her acute *vergüenza* to see me act thus, and that I would never grow up to be a correct *jefe de familia* if I did not know how to be a correct boy. I knew what *vergüenza* was from feeling it time and again; and the notion of growing up to keep a tight rein over a family of my own was somehow satisfying.

42   In our musty apartment in the basement of 418 L, ours remained a Mexican family. I never lost the sense that we were the same, from Jalco to Sacramento. There was the polished cedar box, taken out now and then from the closet to display our heirlooms. I had lost the rifle shells of the revolution, and Tio Tonche, too, was gone. But there was the butterfly sarape, the one I had worn through the Battle of Puebla; a black lace mantilla Doña Henriqueta modeled for us; bits of embroidery and lace she had made; the tin pictures of my grandparents; my report card signed by Señorita Bustamante and Don Salvador; letters from Aunt Esther; and the card with the address of the lady who had kept the Ajax for us. When our mementos were laid out on the bed I plunged my head into the empty box and took deep breaths of the aroma of *puro cedro*, pure Jalcocotán mixed with camphor.

43   We could have hung on the door of our apartment a sign like those we read in some store windows—*Aquí se habla español*. We not only spoke Spanish, we read it. From the *Librería Española*, two blocks up the street, Gustavo and I bought novels for my mother, like *Genoveva de Brabante*, a paperback with the poems of Amado Nervo and a handbook of the history of Mexico. The novels were never read aloud, the poems and the handbook were. Nervo was the famous poet from Tepic, close enough to Jalcocotán to make him our own. And in the history book I learned to read for myself, after many repetitions by my mother, about the deeds of the great Mexicans Don Salvador had recited so vividly to the class in Mazatlán. She refused to decide for me whether Abraham Lincoln was as great as Benito Juarez, or George Washington braver than the priest Don Miguel Hidalgo. At school there was no opportunity to settle these questions because nobody seemed to know about Juarez or Hidalgo; at least they were never mentioned and there were no pictures of them on the walls.

44   The family talk I listened to with the greatest interest was about Jalco. Wherever the conversation began it always turned to the pueblo, our

neighbors, anecdotes that were funny or sad, the folk tales and the witch-craft, and our kinfolk, who were still there. I usually lay on the floor those winter evenings, with my feet toward the kerosene heater, watching on the ceiling the flickering patterns of the light filtered through the scrollwork of the chimney. As I listened once again I chased the *zopilote* away from Coronel, or watched José take Nerón into the forest in a sack. Certain things became clear about the *rurales* and why the young men were taken away to kill Yaqui Indians, and about the Germans, the Englishmen, the Frenchmen, the Spaniards, and the Americans who owned the haciendas, the railroads, the ships, the big stores, the breweries. They owned Mexico because President Porfirio Díaz had let them steal it, José explained as I listened. Now Don Francisco Madero had been assassinated for trying to get it back. On such threads of family talk I followed my own recollection of the years from Jalco—the attack on Mazatlán, the captain of Acaponeta, the camp at El Nanchi and the arrival at Nogales on the flatcar.

45   Only when we ventured uptown did we feel like aliens in a foreign land. Within the *barrio* we heard Spanish on the streets and in the alleys. On the railroad tracks, in the canneries, and along the riverfront there were more Mexicans than any other nationality. And except for the foremen, the work talk was in our language. In the secondhand shops, where the *barrio* people sold and bought furniture and clothing, there were Mexican clerks who knew the Mexican ways of making a sale. Families doubled up in decaying houses, cramping themselves so they could rent an extra room to *chicano* boarders, who accented the brown quality of our Mexican *colonia.* . . .

46   In the *barrio,* music seemed to be everywhere: the records I heard on Mrs. Dodson's victrola; the Sunday concerts of the German brass band; Pork Chops, the black minstrel who played his twelve-string guitar on our sidewalk, humping gently and shuffling as he sang; Frisco at his delirious piano; Miss Florence, pealing out her "Sympathy"; the Slavs, blowing wild melodies through the stops of an accordion that could be heard all over the block.

47   And there was the Salvation Army. They marched down from their headquarters on Sixth and L to Third Street or Second or some other corner where the lower part of town was lowest. In a half circle off the curb they blew their trumpets, pumped their organ, jiggled their tambourines and sang joyously and loudly about Jesus. The pretty girl in the blue dress and the red stripes passed the tambourine for the collection, and contributions were also received on the bass drum, which for the purpose was laid flat on the street.

48   It all led to the purchase of a violin for me so that I, too, could make and not just hear music. We bought it for five dollars at a pawnshop on Fifth Street, and José arranged with a fiddler who played in a saloon to give me two lessons a month for fifty cents.

49   Something remarkable came out of my becoming a violinist. The schools of the city were being requested to recommend candidates for the

Sacramento Boys Band, then being organized. The band needed a piccolo player and Miss Hopley sent my name up as musically and physically equipped for the part.

50   I was accepted into the band, and in that way became the possessor of a short black tube made of hard wood, with holes covered by padded keys operated by tiny brass levers. When I blew on it shrieks came out of the far end. The bandmaster gave me a handbook for the piccolo from which I gradually learned to make my wooden tube trill and pipe above the rest of the band. We toured Davis, Woodland, Lodi, Galt, Marysville, and other towns near Sacramento, dedicating a new milk plant, serenading an important citizen on his birthday, rousing the citizens at rallies, and preparing ourselves to become boy's band champions of the State of California. In one of these contests at the State Fair I conducted the warming up march on a platform in front of the grandstand under a broiling sun. Taking the baton from the master with a bow, I swept the band into "Invercargill," which crashed into the finale several bars ahead of me. Sweating miserably I bowed to the thunder of applause from the grandstand, and sat down. My family were somewhere in the audience.

51   The Y.M.C.A., with the band, opened to me the rest of the wide world around Sacramento. On one side of the new brick building on 5th and J there were posters with boys popping into a swimming pool like frogs and playing ping-pong and handball. There was a conference at 418 L in which my mother, Gustavo, and José, Mrs. Dodson, and Mr. Howard took part. The conclusion was that the "Y" was a good thing, that we had the money, and that I could join. For a dollar I drew my membership pass to the games, the gym class, swimming lessons, and many hours of talk with Chief Wilson, the boy's secretary. In due time he obtained for me a five dollar scholarship for two weeks at summer camp in the Sierras. As a part-time worker I helped clear the camp sites deep in the pine forest and worked my shift in the icy water of a mountain stream raising the dam for our swimming hole.

52   These experiences and new friendships about which my family knew so little and guessed a great deal became the other side of my double life. Gustavo and José were away much of the time but when they were home my education at their hands went on. Gustavo told me endless jokes, like the one about the green *chicano*, fresh from a village like Jalco, who tried to put out the electric light by puffing on it. José sorted out odds and ends of metal, wire, wood, and discards of all sorts, which we kept in a kind of you-never-can-tell box in the back yard. With a pocket knife, a pair of pliers, and a screwdriver we repaired furniture, shoes, clotheslines, iceboxes, and anything else around the house that needed maintenance. We collected useful things the Americans threw away, mechanical gadgets that showed how ingenious they were, and how wasteful, like a discarded alarm clock which we repaired and set up on the kitchen shelf. Watching my uncles test the edge of a sharpened tool, splice a rope, straighten out a nail, whittle a

bottle stopper, or shape a leather sole I was apprenticed to craftsmen who invented as they worked.

from *Barrio Boy* by Ernesto Galarza. Copyright 1971 by the University of Notre Dame Press.

♦ Understanding Each Other: Discussion Questions

1. What is life like in the *barrio* for Ernesto ("Little Ernie") and his family? How is Ernesto's reaction to his environment similar to or different from the reaction of the young boy—as played in the scenario by a member of your class—to his setting?
2. What is Lincoln School like? What are Ernesto's teachers like? How does he feel about them? What was your first American school like? Are there any similarities between it and Lincoln School? What were your teachers like? How do you feel about them?
3. How many other nationalities, besides Mexican Americans, also live in the *barrio*? Describe three or four characters—each from a different country. Do you live in a similar neighborhood? Do you have friends from other countries outside of school?
4. List five *adjectives* which describe Doña Henriqueta, Ernesto's mother. How do you think your mother would react in the same situations? Would you want her to behave differently?

5. What differences in behavior and customs between Americans and Mexicans does Ernesto mention? What differences have you noticed?

6. List all of the musical instruments which Galarza mentions in his story. Which ones does Ernesto play? Do you play any of them? Do you play any other instrument?

7. To add to the family income, Ernesto takes a variety of jobs. Do you think he should have undertaken these kinds of jobs? What would you have done?

8. Galarza has made several allusions in this excerpt. Use an encyclopedia and an English-English dictionary to identify the following: Sutter's Fort; King Arthur; Columbus; Buffalo Bill; Daniel Boone; Sumo; an Erector set; pig-Latin; Amado Nervo; Abraham Lincoln; Benito Juarez; George Washington; Don Miguel Hidalgo; President Porfirio Díaz; and the Salvation Army.

9. What kind of an education does Ernesto get from the *barrio*? Be sure to describe and discuss Ernesto's gang. What has your American experience taught you?

10. What is your opinion of the characters' attitudes toward and attempts to speak American English? Who insists that proper Spanish be spoken? Is that a correct point of view in your opinion? How does age affect attitudes toward speaking English among Ernesto's family members and friends? How does facility with American English shift the balance of power inside the family? Have you or your family had any experiences similar to these?

◆ Interactive Grammar and Usage: Rules in Reflection

With a partner, practice idiomatic usage in English by filling in the blanks below with correct word choices. Your teacher may give you a list of possible answers. Your goal is to make a coherent and cohesive passage. Some of the choices are those found in the reading; others are close in meaning. Be prepared to explain the reasons for each answer. Then formulate the grammatical rules which are implicit here, based on what you have observed. The first sentence is completed for you as an example.

Our family <u>conversations</u> always occurred on our kitchen porch, away <u>from</u> the gringos. One or the other of the adults _____ begin: <u>Se</u> 1

<u>han fijado?</u> Had _____ noticed—that the Americans do 2

_____ ask permission _____ leave the room; that they 3   4

had _____ respectful way of addressing _____ elderly 5   6

person; that _____ spit brown _____ the railing of the 7   8

_____ into the yard; that _____ they laughed they
    9   10

roared; _____ they never brought <u>saludos</u> to everyone
          11

_____ your family from everyone in their family when they vis-
  12

ited; that <u>General Delibree</u> was only _____ clerk; that <u>zopilotes</u>
                           13

_____ not allowed on the streets to collect garbage; that
  14

_____ policemen _____ not carry lanterns at night; that
  15   16

Americans didn't keep _____ feet on the floor when they were
                17

_____; that there was a special _____ for going to jail;
  18   19

that a rancho was _____ a rancho at all _____ a very small
           20   21

hacienda; that _____ saloons served their _____ free
          22   23

eggs, pickles, _____ sandwiches; that instead _____
          24   25

bullfighting, the gringos for sport _____ to kill each
                      26

_____ with gloves?
  27

◆ Increasing Word Power: Vocabulary in Context

Working with a partner, decide on the meaning *in context* of each of the following words or phrases. Then look up each item in a good English-English
dictionary. Does the context meaning of the word in the reading differ in
any way from the dictionary's definition? If so, how did the context help
you understand the meaning of the word as used in the passage?

Word	Meaning in This Context	Dictionary Definition
barrio		
scribbles		
kaleidoscope		
canneries		
warehouse		
kilns		
smithies		
drays		
honking		
nipped		
gunnysack		
gleanings		
griddle		
roasted		

Word	Meaning in This Context	Dictionary Definition
scrubbing		
down quilt		
scroll		
taunts		
adjoining		
mourned		
naturalist		
methodically		
handbills		
skid row		
brawl		
smudged		
stool pigeon		
vigilante		
no-man's-land		
nook		
swagger		
underworld		
pilfering		
raid		
brayed		
embroidery		
filtered		
pawnshop		
serenading		
apprenticed		

♦ Finding Your Own Voice: For Discussion and Writing

1. Discuss your reaction to this story. Here are some questions you might address.

   What do you think of this story?
   Were you touched by it?
   Which character did you like the best? Why?
   Which character did you like the least? Why?
   What do you think will happen next to Ernesto?

2. Describe your own experiences or those of your child in an American school. Write a story or essay.

3. How does your concept of friendship compare with that of the narrator in the story? Define your concept in a story or an essay.

4. Discuss the importance of friendships in your country. Are men friends? Can men and women have friendships there? Write a story or essay.
5. Perform the scenario "Business is business" to bring your work with this chapter full circle. Your teacher may ask you to write an essay about the theme of this scenario, by yourself or with other students.

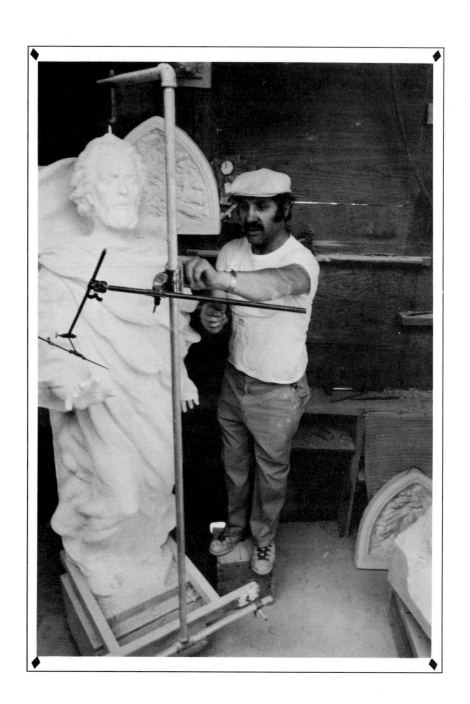

CHAPTER 6

Italian American

◆ Listening to Each Other: Scenario

See Chapter 1 for instructions on how to perform a scenario.

Prepare and perform the scenario "A dangerous situation." If there is time, also perform the scenario "Family decisions."

◆ Speaking Out: Debriefing Questions

1. Discuss the reaction to the job conditions of each person in the scenario.
2. What are the problems which each character faces?
3. Who had solutions for his or her own problems? For the family's problems?
4. How important is education to each of the characters?
5. With which character in the scenario did you identify? Explain why you empathized with that person.
6. Would you change anything if the scenario were acted out again?

◆ Reaching Out: Suggestions for Further Activities

1. Reverse the roles: have the father play the part of the job foreman and vice versa; then have the father play the part of the son and vice versa.
2. Create another scenario, in which the whole class organizes a union to fight for better working conditions. Then write an essay about one aspect of this scenario and bring it into class for the group to critique and polish.

3. Research the labor-union movement in the United States. If there are some local labor unions in your city, interview one of the leaders and ask about the history of that organization. Then prepare and present a short talk about that union, or about unions in general, for your classmates.
4. Go to a library and find a book about the contributions of Italian Americans to the growth and development of the United States. In which areas were and are these contributions *especially* significant?
5. If possible, watch the movie *Moonstruck.* Take notes on the lifestyles of these Italian Americans and on the kinds of problems they face. If you are of Italian extraction, discuss with your classmates how realistic you found the movie. After reading the excerpt from Di Donato, compare the experiences of the film characters with those of Di Donato's characters.

♦ Reading: From *Christ in Concrete*, by Pietro Di Donato

Read the following selection, keeping in mind the scenario you have already experienced. It is always a good idea to have an English-English dictionary at hand when you read. A useful technique is to read the selection through quickly the first time, highlighting words or phrases that you think you need to look up. Then go back and do a more careful reading, looking up unfamiliar words.

1

1   March whistled stinging snow against the brick walls and up the gaunt girders. Geremio, the foreman, swung his arms about, and gaffed the men on.

2   Old Nick, the "Lean," stood up from over a dust-flying brick pile, tapped the side of his nose and sent an oyster directly to the ground. "Master Geremio, the Devil himself could not break his tail any harder than we here."

3   Burly Julio of the walrus mustache and known as the "Snoutnose" let fall the chute door of the concrete hopper and sang over in the Lean's direction: "Mari-Annina's belly and the burning night will make of me once more a milk-mouthed stripling lad . . ."

4   The Lean loaded his wheelbarrow and spat furiously. "Sons of two-legged dogs . . . despised of even the Devil himself! Work! Sure! For America beautiful will eat you and spit your bones into the earth's hole! Work!" And with that his wiry frame pitched the barrow violently over the rough floor.

5   Snoutnose waved his head to and fro and with mock pathos wailed, "Sing on, O guitar of mine . . ."

6   Short, cheery-faced Tomas, the scaffoldman, paused with hatchet in hand and tenpenny spike sticking out from small dicelike teeth to tell the

Lean as he went by, in a voice that all could hear, "Ah, father of countless chicks, the old age is a carrion!"

7 Geremio chuckled and called to him. "Hey, little Tomas, who are you to talk? You and big-titted Cola can't even hatch an egg, whereas the Lean has just to turn the door-knob of his bedroom and old Philomena becomes a balloon!"

8 Coarse throats tickled and mouths opened wide in laughter.

9 The Lean pushed his barrow on, his face cruelly furrowed with time and struggle. Sirupy sweat seeped from beneath his cap, down his bony nose and turned icy at its end. He muttered to himself. "Saints up, down, sideways and inside out! How many more stones must I carry before I'm overstuffed with the light of day! I don't understand . . . blood of the Virgin, I don't understand!"

10 Mike the "Barrel-mouth" pretended he was talking to himself and yelled out in his best English . . . he was always speaking English while the rest carried on in their native Italian. "I don't know myself, but somebodys whose gotta bigga buncha keeds and he alla times talka from somebodys elsa!"

11 Geremio knew it was meant for him and he laughed. "On the tomb of Saint Pimple-legs, this little boy my wife is giving me next week shall be the last! Eight hungry little Christians to feed is enough for any man."

12 Tomas nodded to the rest. "Sure, Master Geremio had a telephone call from the next bambino. Yes, it told him it had a little bell between instead of a rose bush . . . . It even told him its name!"

13 "Laugh, laugh all of you," returned Geremio, "but I tell you that all my kids must be boys so that they someday will be big American builders. And then I'll help them to put the gold away in the basements!"

14 A great din of riveting shattered the talk among the fast-moving men. Geremio added a handful of Honest tobacco to his corncob, puffed strongly, and cupped his hands around the bowl for a bit of warmth. The chill day caused him to shiver, and he thought to himself: Yes, the day is cold, cold . . . but who am I to complain when the good Christ Himself was crucified?

15 Pushing the job is all right (when has it been otherwise in my life?), but this job frightens me. I feel the building wants to tell me something; just as one Christian to another. Or perhaps the Easter week is making of me a spirit-seeing pregnant woman. I don't like this. Mr. Murdin tells me, Push it up! That's all he knows. I keep telling him that the underpinning should be doubled and the old material removed from the floors, but he keeps the inspector drunk and . . . "Hey, Ashes-ass! Get away from under that pilaster! Don't pull the old work. Push it away from you or you'll have a nice present for Easter if the wall falls on you!" . . . Well, with the help of God I'll see this job through. It's not my first, nor the . . . "Hey, Patsy number two! Put more cement in that concrete; we're putting up a building, not an Easter cake!"

16   Patsy hurled his shovel to the floor and gesticulated madly. "The padrone Murdin-sa tells me, 'Too much, too much! Lil' bit is plenty!' And you tell me I'm stingy! The rotten building can fall after I leave!"

17   Six floors below, the contractor called. "Hey, Geremio! Is your gang of dagos dead?"

18   Geremio cautioned the men. "On your toes, boys. If he writes out slips, someone won't have big eels on the Easter table."

19   The Lean cursed that the padrone could take the job and all the Saints for that matter and shove it . . . !

20   Curly-headed Lazarene, the roguish, pigeon-toed scaffoldman, spat a cloud of tobacco juice and hummed to his own music . . . "Yes, certainly yes to your face, master padrone . . . and behind, This to you and all your kind!"

21   The day, like all days, came to an end. Calloused and bruised bodies sighed, and numb legs shuffled toward shabby railroad flats . . .

22   "Ah, bella casa mio. Where my little freshets of blood and my good woman await me. Home where my broken back will not ache so. Home where midst the monkey chatter of my piccolinos I will float off to blessed slumber with my feet on the chair and the head on the wife's soft full breast."

23   These great child-hearted ones leave one another without words or ceremony, and as they ride and walk home, a great pride swells the breast . . .

24   "Blessings to Thee, O Jesus. I have fought winds and cold. Hand to hand I have locked dumb stones in place and the great building rises. I have earned a bit of bread for me and mine."

25   The mad day's brutal conflict is forgiven, and strained limbs prostrate themselves so that swollen veins can send the yearning blood coursing and pulsating deliciously as though the body mountained leaping streams.

26   The job alone remained behind . . . and yet, they also, having left the bigger part of their lives with it. The cold ghastly beast, the Job, stood stark, the eerie March wind wrapping it in sharp shadows of falling dusk.

27   That night was a crowning point in the life of Geremio. He bought a house! Twenty years he had helped to mold the New World. And now he was to have a house of his own! What mattered that it was no more than a wooden shack? It was his own!

28   He had proudly signed his name and helped Annunziata to make her X on the wonderful contract that proved them owners. And she was happy to think that her next child, soon to come, would be born under their own rooftree. She heard the church chimes, and cried to the children, "Children, to bed! It is near midnight. And remember, shut-mouth to the paesanos! Or they will send the evil eye to our new home even before we put foot."

29   The children scampered off to the icy yellow bedroom where three slept in one bed and three in the other. Coltishly and friskily they kicked about under the covers; their black iron-cotton stockings not removed . . . what! and freeze the peanut-little toes?

30   Said Annunziata, "The children are so happy, Geremio; let them be, for even I would dance a Tarantella." And with that she turned blushing. He

wanted to take her on her word. She patted his hands, kissed them, and whispered. "Our children will dance for us . . . in the American style someday."

31 Geremio cleared his throat and wanted to sing. "Yes, with joy I could sing in a richer feeling than the great Caruso." He babbled little old-country couplets and circled the room until the tenant below tapped the ceiling.

32 Annunziata whispered, "Geremio, to bed and rest. Tomorrow is a day for great things . . . and the day on which our Lord died for us."

33 The children were now hard asleep. Heads under the cover, over . . . snotty noses whistling, and little damp legs entwined.

34 In bed Geremio and Annunziata clung closely to each other. They mumbled figures and dates until fatigue stilled their thoughts. And with chubby Johnny clutching fast his bottle and warmed between them . . . life breathed heavily, and dreams entertained in far, far worlds, the nation-builder's brood.

35 But Geremio and Annunziata remained for a long while staring into the darkness . . . silently.

36 At last Annunziata spoke. "Geremio?"

"Yes?"

"This job you are now working . . ."

"So?"

"You used always to tell me about what happened on the jobs . . . who was jealous, and who praised . . ."

"You should know by now that all work is the same . . ."

"Geremio. The month you have been on this job, you have not spoken a word about the work . . . And I have felt that I am walking into a dream. Is the work dangerous? Why don't you answer . . .?"

2

37 Job loomed up damp, shivery gray. Its giant members waiting.

38 Builders donned their coarse robes, and waited.

39 Geremio's whistle rolled back into his pocket and the symphony of struggle began.

40 Trowel rang through brick and slashed mortar rivets were machine-gunned fast with angry grind Patsy number one check Patsy number two check the Lean three Julio four steel bellowed back at hammer donkey engines coughed purple Ashes-ass Pietro fifteen chisel point intoned stone thin steel whirred and wailed through wood liquid stone flowed with dull rasp through iron veins and hoist screamed through space Rosario the Fat twenty-four and Giacomo Sangini check . . . The multitudinous voices of a civilization rose from the surroundings and melted with the efforts of the Job.

41 The Lean as he fought his burden on looked forward to only one goal, the end. The barrow he pushed, he did not love. The stones that brutalized his palms, he did not love. The great God Job, he did not love. He felt a searing bitterness and a fathomless consternation at the queer conscious-

ness that inflicted the ever mounting weight of structures that he *had to! had to!* raise about his shoulders! When, when and where would the last stone be? Never . . . did he bear his toil with the rhythm of song! Never . . . did his gasping heart knead the heavy mortar with lilting melody! A voice within him spoke in wordless language.

42 The language of worn oppression and the despair of realizing that his life had been left on brick piles. And always, there had been hunger and her bastard, the fear of hunger.

43 Murdin bore down upon Geremio from behind and shouted:

44 "Goddammit, Geremio, if you're givin' the men two hours off today with pay, why the hell are they draggin' their tails? And why don't you turn that skinny old Nick loose, and put a young wop in his place?"

45 "Now listen-a to me, Mister Murdin—"

"Don't give me that! And bear in mind that there are plenty of good barefoot men in the streets who'll jump for a day's pay!"

"Padrone—padrone, the underpinning gotta be make safe and . . ."

"Lissenyawopbastard! if you don't like it, you know what you can do!" And with that he swung swaggering away.

46 The men had heard, and those who hadn't knew instinctively.

47 The new home, the coming baby, and his whole background, kept the fire from Geremio's mouth and bowed his head. "Annunziata speaks of scouring the ashcans for the children's bread in case I didn't want to work on a job where . . . . But am I not a man, to feed my own with these hands? Ah, but day will end and no boss in the world can then rob me the joy of my home!"

48 Murdin paused for a moment before descending the ladder.

49 Geremio caught his meaning and jumped to, nervously directing the rush of work . . . . No longer Geremio, but a machinelike entity.

50 The men were transformed into single, silent beasts. Snoutnose steamed through ragged mustache whip-lashing sand into mixer Ashes-ass dragged under four-by-twelve beam Lean clawed wall knots jumping in jaws masonry crumbled dust billowed thundered choked . . .

51 At noon, dripping noses were blown, old coats thrown over shoulders, and foot-long sandwiches were toasted at the end of wire over the flames. Shadows were once again personalities. Laughter added warmth.

52 Geremio drank his wine from an old-fashioned magnesia bottle and munched a great pepper sandwich . . . no meat on Good Friday.

53 Said one, "Are some of us to be laid off? Easter is upon us and communion dresses are needed and . . ."

54 That, while Geremio was dreaming of the new house and the joys he could almost taste. Said he, "Worry not. You should know Geremio." It then all came out. He regaled them with his wonderful joy of the new house. He praised his wife and children one by one. They listened respectfully and returned him well wishes and blessings. He went on and on . . . . "Paul made a radio—all by himself, mind you! One can hear *Barney Google* and many American songs!"

55   "A radio!"

"An electric machine like magic—yes."

"With music and Christian voices?"

"That is nothing to what he shall someday accomplish!"

"Who knows," suggested Giacomo amazed, "but that Dio has deigned to gift you with a Marconi . . ."

"I tell you, son of Geremio shall never never lay bricks! Paulie mine will study from books—he will be the great builder! This very moment I can see him . . . How proud he!"

Said they in turn: "Master Geremio, in my province it is told that for good luck in a new home, one is to sprinkle well with salt . . . especially the corners, and on moving day sweep with a new broom to the center and pick all up—but do not sweep it out over the threshold!"

"That may be, Pietro. But, Master Geremio, it would be better in my mind that holy water should bless. And also a holy picture of Saint Joseph guarding the door."

"The Americans use the shoe of a horse . . . there must be something in that. One may try . . ."

56   Snoutnose knew a better way. "You know, you know." He ogled his eyes and smacked his lips. Then, reaching out his hands over the hot embers . . . "To embrace a goose-fat breast and bless the house with the fresh milk. And one that does not belong to the wife . . . that is the way!"

57   Acid-smelling di Nobilis were lit. Geremio preferred his corncob. And Lazarene "tobacco-eater" proudly chawed his quid . . . in the American style.

58   The ascent to labor was made, and as they trod the ladder, heads turned and eyes communed with the mute flames of the brazier whose warmth they were leaving, not with willing heart, and in that fleeting moment the breast wanted much to speak of hungers that never reached the tongue.

59   About an hour later, Geremio called over to Pietro, "Pietro, see if Mister Murdin is in the shanty and tell him I must see him! I will convince him that the work must not go on like this . . . just for the sake of a little more profit!"

60   Pietro came up soon. "The padrone is not coming up. He was drinking from a large bottle of whisky and cursed in American words that if you did not carry out his orders—"

61   Geremio turned away disconcerted, stared dumbly at the structure and mechanically listed in his mind's eye the various violations of construction safety. An uneasy sensation hollowed him. The Lean brought down an old piece of wall and the structure palsied. Geremio's heart broke loose and out-thumped the floor's vibrations, a rapid wave of heat swept him and left a chill touch in its wake. He looked about to the men, a bit frightened. They seemed usual, life-size, and moved about with the methodical deftness that made the moment then appear no different than the task of toil had ever been.

62   Snoutnose's voice boomed into him. "Master Geremio, the concrete is re-ady!"

63   "Oh yes, yes, Julio." And he walked gingerly toward the chute, but not without leaving behind some part of his strength, sending out his soul to wrestle with the limbs of Job, who threatened in stiff silence. He talked and joked with Snoutnose. Nothing said anything, nor seemed wrong. Yet a vague uneasiness was to him as certain as the foggy murk that floated about Job's stone and steel.

64   "Shall I let the concrete down now, Master Geremio?"

"Well, let me see—no, hold it a minute. Hey, Lazarene! Tighten the chute cables!"

65   Snoutnose straightened, looked about, and instinctively rubbed the sore small of his spine. "Ah," sighed he, "all the men feel as I—yes, I can tell. They are tired but happy that today is Good Friday and we quit at three o'clock—" And he swelled in human ecstasy at the anticipation of food, drink and the hairy flesh-tingling warmth of wife, and then, extravagant rest.

66   Geremio gazed about and was conscious of seeming to understand many things. He marveled at the strange feeling which permitted him to sense the familiarity of life. And yet—all appeared unreal, a dream pungent and nostalgic.

67   Life, dream, reality, unreality, spiraling ever about each other. "Ha," he chuckled, "how and from where do these thoughts come?"

68   Snoutnose had his hand on the hopper latch and was awaiting the word from Geremio. "Did you say something, Master Geremio?"

69   "Why yes, Julio, I was thinking—funny! A—yes, what is the time—yes, that is what I was thinking."

"My American can of tomatoes says ten minutes from two o'clock. It won't be long now, Master Geremio."

Geremio smiled. "No, about an hour . . . and then, home."

"Oh, but first we stop at Mulberry Street, to buy their biggest eels, and the other finger-licking stuffs."

70   Geremio was looking far off, and for a moment happiness came to his heart without words, a warm hand stealing over. Snoutnose's words sang to him pleasantly, and he nodded.

71   "And Master Geremio, we ought really to buy the sea-fruits with the shells—you know, for the much needed steam they put into the—"

72   He flushed despite himself and continued, "It is true, I know it— especially the juicy clams . . . uhmn, my mouth waters like a pump."

73   Geremio drew on his unlit pipe and smiled acquiescence. The men around him were moving to their tasks silently, feeling of their fatigue, but absorbed in contemplations the very same as Snoutnose's. The noise of labor seemed not to be noise, and as Geremio looked about, life settled over him a gray concert—gray forms, atmosphere and gray notes . . . . Yet his off-tone world felt so near, and familiar.

74   "Five minutes from two," swished through Snoutnose's mustache.

75   Geremio automatically took out his watch, rewound and set it. Lazarene had done with the cables. The tone and movement of the scene seemed to

Geremio strange, differently strange, and yet, a dream familiar from a timeless date. His hand went up in motion to Julio. The molten stone gurgled low, and then with heightening rasp. His eyes followed the stone-cementy pudding, and to his ears there was no other sound than its flow. From over the roofs somewhere, the tinny voice of *Barney Google* whined its way, hooked into his consciousness and kept itself a revolving record beneath his skullplate.

76   "Ah, yes, *Barney Google,* my son's wonderful radio machine . . . wonderful Paul." His train of thought quickly took in his family, home and hopes. And with hope came fear. Something within asked, "Is it not possible to breathe God's air without fear dominating with the pall of unemployment? And the terror of production for Boss, Boss and Job? To rebel is to lose all of the very little. To be obedient is to choke. O dear Lord, guide my path."

77   Just then, the floor lurched and swayed under his feet. The slipping of the underpinning below rumbled up through the undetermined floors.

78   Was he faint or dizzy? Was it part of the dreamy afternoon? He put his hands in front of him and stepped back, and looked up wildly. "No! No!"

79   The men poised stricken. Their throats wanted to cry out and scream but didn't dare. For a moment they were a petrified and straining pageant. Then the bottom of their world gave way. The building shuddered violently, her supports burst with the crackling slap of wooden gunfire. The floor vomited upward. Geremio clutched at the air and shrieked agonizingly. "Brothers, what have we done? Ahhh-h, children of ours!" With the speed of light, balance went sickeningly awry and frozen men went flying explosively. Job tore down upon them madly. Walls, floors, beams became whirling, solid, splintering waves crashing with detonations that ground man and material in bonds of death.

80   The strongly shaped body that slept with Annunziata nights and was perfect in all the limitless physical quantities thudded as a worthless sack amongst the giant débris that crushed fragile flesh and bone with centrifugal intensity.

81   Darkness blotted out his terror and the resistless form twisted, catapulted insanely in its directionless flight, and shot down neatly and deliberately between the empty wooden forms of a foundation wall pilaster in upright position, his blue swollen face pressed against the form and his arms outstretched, caught securely through the meat by the thin round bars of reinforcing steel.

82   The huge concrete hopper that was sustained by an independent structure of thick timber wavered a breath or so, its heavy concrete rolling uneasily until a great sixteen-inch wall caught it squarely with all the terrific verdict of its dead weight and impelled it downward through joists, beams and masonry until it stopped short, arrested by two girders, an arm's length above Geremio's head; the gray concrete gushing from the hopper mouth, and sealing up the mute figure.

83   Giacomo had been thrown clear of the building and dropped six floors to the street gutter, where he lay writhing.

84   The Lean had evinced no emotion. When the walls descended, he did not move. He lowered his head. One minute later he was hanging in mid-air, his chin on his chest, his eyes tearing loose from their sockets, a green foam bubbling from his mouth and his body spasming, suspended by the shreds left of his mashed arms, pinned between a wall and a girder.

85   A two-by-four hooked little Tomas up under the back of his jumper and swung him around in a circle to meet a careening I-beam. In the flash that he lifted his frozen cherubic face, its shearing edge sliced through the top of his skull.

86   When Snoutnose cried beseechingly, "Saint Michael!" blackness enveloped him. He came to in a world of horror. A steady stream, warm, thick, and sickening as hot wine, bathed his face and clogged his nose, mouth, and eyes. The nauseous sirup that pumped over his face clotted his mustache red and drained into his mouth. He gulped for air, and swallowed blood. As he breathed, the pain shocked him to oppressive semiconsciousness. The air was wormingly alive with cries, screams, moans, and dust, and his crushed chest seared him with a thousand fires. He couldn't see, nor breathe enough to cry. His right hand moved to his face and wiped at the gelatinizing substance, but it kept coming on, and a heartbreaking moan wavered about him, not far. He wiped his eyes in subconscious despair. Where was he? What kind of a dream was he having? Perhaps he wouldn't wake up in time for work, and then what? But how queer; his stomach beating him, his chest on fire, he sees nothing but dull red, only one hand moving about, and a moaning in his face!

87   The sound and clamor of the rescue squads called to him from far off.

88   Ah, yes, he's dreaming in bed, and, far out in the streets, engines are going to a fire. Oh, poor devils! Suppose his house were on fire? With the children scattered about in the rooms he could not remember! He must do his utmost to break out of this dream! He's swimming under water, not able to raise his head and get to the air. He must get back to consciousness to save his children!

89   He swam frantically with his one right hand, and then felt a face beneath its touch. A face! It's Angelina alongside of him! Thank God, he's awake! He tapped her face. It moved. It felt cold, bristly, and wet. "It moves so. What is this?" His fingers slithered about grisly sharp bones and in a gluey, stringy, hollow mass, yielding as wet macaroni. Gray light brought sight, and hysteria punctured his heart. A girder lay across his chest, his right hand clutched a grotesque human mask, and suspended almost on top of him was the twitching, faceless body of Tomas. Julio fainted with an inarticulate sigh. His fingers loosed and the bodiless headless face dropped and fitted to the side of his face while the drippings above came slower and slower.

90   The rescue men cleaved grimly with pick and ax.

91   Geremio came to with a start . . . far from their efforts. His brain told him instantly what had happened and where he was. He shouted wildly. "Save me! Save me! I'm being buried alive!"

92 He paused exhausted. His genitals convulsed. The cold steel rod upon which they were impaled froze his spine. He shouted louder and louder. "Save me! I am hurt badly! I can be saved I can—save me before it's too late!" But the cries went no farther than his own ears. The icy wet concrete reached his chin. His heart appalled. "In a few seconds I will be entombed. If I can only breathe, they will reach me. Surely, they will!" His face was quickly covered, its flesh yielding to the solid sharp-cut stones. "Air! Air!" screamed his lungs as he was completely sealed. Savagely he bit into the wooden form pressed upon his mouth. An eighth of an inch of its surface splintered off. Oh, if he could only hold out long enough to bite even the smallest hole through to air! He must! There can be no other way! He must! There can be no other way! He is responsible for his family! He cannot leave them like this! He didn't want to die! This could not be the answer to life! He had bitten halfway through when his teeth snapped off to the gums in the uneven conflict. The pressure of the concrete was such, and its effectiveness so thorough, that the wooden splinters, stumps of teeth, and blood never left the choking mouth.

93 Why couldn't he go any farther?

94 Air! Quick! He dug his lower jaw into the little hollowed space and gnashed in choking agonized fury. Why doesn't it go through! Mother of Christ, why doesn't it give? Can there be a notch, or two-by-four stud behind it? Sweet Jesu! No! No! Make it give . . . Air! Air!

95 He pushed the bone-bare jaw maniacally; it splintered, cracked, and a jagged fleshless edge cut through the form, opening a small hole to air. With a desperate burst the lung-prisoned air blew an opening through the shredded mouth and whistled back greedily a gasp of fresh air. He tried to breathe, but it was impossible. The heavy concrete was settling immutably and its rich cement-laden grout ran into his pierced face. His lungs would not expand and were crushing in tighter and tighter under the settling concrete.

96 "Mother mine—mother of Jesu—Annunziata—children of mine—dear, dear, for mercy, Jesu-Giuseppe e' Mari," his blue foamed tongue called. It then distorted in a shuddering coil and mad blood vomited forth. Chills and fire played through him and his tortured tongue stuttered, "Mercy, blessed Father—salvation, most kind Father—Saviour—Saviour of His children, help me—adored Saviour—I kiss your feet eternally—you are my Lord—there is but one God—you are my God of infinite mercy—Hail Mary divine Virgin—our Father who art in heaven hallowed be thy— name—our Father—my Father," and the agony excruciated with never-ending mount, "our Father—Jesu, Jesu, soon Jesu, hurry dear Jesu Jesu! Jesssu . . . !" His mangled voice trebled hideously, and hung in jerky whimperings. Blood vessels burst like mashed flower stems. He screamed. "Show yourself now, Jesu! Now is the time! Save me! Why don't you come! Are you there! I cannot stand it—ohhh, why do you let it happen—where are you? Hurry hurry hurry!"

97   His bones cracked mutely and his sanity went sailing distorted in the limbo of the subconscious. With the throbbing tones of an organ in the hollow background, the fighting brain disintegrated and the memories of a baffled lifetime sought outlet.

98   He moaned the simple songs of barefoot childhood, scenes flashed desperately on and off, and words and parts of words came pitifully high and low from his inaudible lips.

99   Paul's crystal-set earphones pressed the sides of his head tighter and tighter, the organ boomed the mad dance of the Tarentella, and the hysterical mind sang cringingly and breathlessly, "Jesu my Lord my God my all Jesu my Lord my God my all Jesu my Lord my God my all Jesu my Lord my God my all."

from Di Donato, Pietro. *Christ in Concrete*. Indianapolis: The Bobbs-Merrill Company, 1939. Reprinted with permission of Macmillan Publishing Co. Copyright renewed 1967 by Pietro Di Donato.

♦ Understanding Each Other: Discussion Questions

1. Describe in detail the conditions under which Geremio and his fellow construction workers have to do their jobs. Do you think such conditions still prevail today?

2. What kind of a man is Geremio? List five *adjectives* which describe his personality. What would you do in Geremio's place?
3. Why is having their own home so important to Geremio and Annunziata? What does it symbolize? Do you feel the same way about owning a house?
4. What is a *godfather*? A *padrone*? Do you have any similar relationships in your country?
5. When authors let the reader inside the minds of characters, they are using a technique called "stream of consciousness." What effect on *your* feelings does being inside Geremio's mind have?
6. Of what significance is the dance, the *tarantella*, in Annunziata's life? How important is dancing to Italians? Is dancing important in your country? Do women dance with both men *and* women? Do men dance with both men *and* women?
7. What does "the Job" mean to Geremio? To Paul? And to you?
8. What are the conflicts in this story? Identify as many as you can. How are they resolved? Do you find similar conflicts in life today?
9. How does the author handle the theme of the struggle to survive? How universal is this theme?
10. What are conditions like for laborers in the United States today? What are conditions like for laborers in your native country?

◆ Interactive Grammar and Usage: Rules in Reflection

With a peer, practice standard English usage by filling in the blanks from the choices your teacher gives you. Make a coherent and cohesive passage. Some of the choices are those found in the reading; others are close in meaning. Be prepared to explain the reasons for your choices. Formulate the rules of grammar and usage implicit here. The first sentence is done for you.

That night was a crowning point <u>in</u> the life <u>of</u> Geremio. He _____₁ a house! Twenty years he _____₂ helped to mold _____₃ New World. _____₄ now _____₅ was to have a _____₆ of his own! What mattered that _____₇ was no more _____₈ a wooden shack? _____₉ was his own!

He had proudly signed _____₁₀ name and helped Annunziata to make _____₁₁ X on the wonderful _____₁₂ that proved them owners. And she was _____₁₃ to think that her next child, soon to come, would _____₁₄ born _____₁₅ their own rooftree. _____₁₆ heard the church chimes, and _____₁₇ to the chil-

dren, "Children, to bed! It is _____ midnight. And remember,
18

shut-mouth to _____ paesanos! Or they _____ send the
19   20

evil eye to our _____ home even before we put foot."
21

The children scampered off _____ the icy yellow bedroom
22

_____ three slept in one _____ and three _____
23   24   25

the other. Coltishly and friskily they _____ about under the cov-
26

ers; _____ black iron-cotton stockings not removed . . . what! and
27

freeze the peanut-little _____ ?
28

◆ Increasing Word Power: Vocabulary in Context

Working with a partner, decide on the meaning *in context* of each of the following words or phrases. Then look up each item in a good English-English
dictionary. Does the context meaning of the word in the reading differ in
any way from the dictionary's definition? If so, how did the context help
you understand the meaning of the word as used in the passage?

Word	Meaning in This Context	Dictionary Definition
gaunt		
gaffed		
walrus		
wheelbarrow		
wiry		
mock pathos		
scaffoldman		
carrion		
bambino		
riveting		
shiver		
gesticulated		
brood		
scampered		
rasp		
babbled		
swaggering		
mute		
disconcerted		
pungent		
nostalgic		
acquiescence		

Word	Meaning in This Context	Dictionary Definition
evinced		
limbo		
disintegrated		
baffled		
cringingly		
terra-cotta		
jaunty		
feigns		
quailed		
resurging		
maelstrom		
convolutions		
parapet		
numbing		
votive		
lume		
crucifix		
garlanded		

◆ Finding Your Own Voice: For Discussion and Writing

1. What is your reaction to this story? Here are some questions to assist you in expressing your reaction:

   Did you like this story? Why?
   Did you find anything shocking?
   How realistic is this story in today's society?
   Were you moved by what happens to the family members?
   Which character did you like the *most*? Why?
   Which character did you like the *least*? Why?
   What do you think Paul, Geremio's eldest, will do now?

2. Discuss your own experiences on your first job in the United States (or discuss the experiences of a relative). Compare your working conditions (or your relative's) to the conditions under which Geremio had to work. Write a story or essay.

3. Describe your hopes and dreams for your *own* children.

4. Perform the scenario "Taking a risk" to bring your work with this chapter full circle. Your teacher may ask you to write an essay about the theme of this scenario, by yourself or with other students.

CHAPTER 7

Japanese American

♦ Listening to Each Other: Scenario

See Chapter 1 for instructions on how to perform a scenario.

Prepare and perform the scenario "Torn by two loyalties." If there is time, also perform the scenario "A delicate matter."

♦ Speaking Out: Debriefing Questions

1. Discuss the reaction of the people in the scenario to the situation that confronts them. How did the parents handle this situation? What advice did they each give to their children?
2. What do you think will happen when the older child returns to school? When the younger child returns to school?
3. What advice would you give to the children if the scenario were presented again?
4. If you could play a role other than the one you were assigned, either as a direct participant or as a member of the support group, which one would you choose?

♦ Reaching Out: Suggestions for Further Activities

1. Some Japanese Americans were confined to internment camps during World War II. What would you have done if you had been responsibile for deciding what to do with them? Create a scenario in which one role

is that of a young Japanese American student who is returning to school after the war and the other role is that of a teacher who is assigned to help the student readjust to school.

2. Descendants of Japanese immigrants have made significant contributions to American society and to American culture. Go to the library and do some research on these contributions. If possible, talk to a second-or third-generation Japanese American to get that person's point of view.

3. What is a *multicultural* person? Define this term and then decide whether or not you are a multicultural person. Do you think being multicultural just means knowing more than one language?

4. If possible, watch the movie, *Sayonara*. What reactions toward cultural differences do you see among the major characters in the story? Among the minor characters? In the background during the story? What kinds of discrimination are present in the cultures represented in the film? Take notes which can be used later in a cause-and-effect writing assignment.

◆ Reading: From *Yokohama, California,* by Toshio Mori

Read the following selection, keeping in mind the scenario you have already experienced. It is always a good idea to have an English-English dictionary at hand when you read. A useful technique is to read the selection through quickly the first time, highlighting words or phrases that you think you need to look up. Then go back and do a more careful reading, looking up unfamiliar words.

TOMORROW IS COMING, CHILDREN

1   Long ago, children, I lived in a country called Japan. Your grandpa was already in California earning money for my boat ticket. The village people rarely went out of Japan and were shocked when they heard I was following your grandpa as soon as the money came.

2   "America!" they cried. "America is on the other side of the world! You will be in a strange country. You cannot read or write their language. What will you do?" I smiled, and in my dreams I saw the San Francisco your grandpa wrote about: San Francisco, the city with strange enticing food; the city with gold coins; the city with many strange faces and music; the city with great buildings and ships.

3   One day his letter came with the money. "Come at once," he wrote. "Don't delay." The neighbors rushed excitedly to the house. "Don't go! Live among us," they cried. "There will be war between America and Japan. You will be caught in mid-Pacific. You will never reach America." But I was determined. They painted the lonely lives of immigrants in a strange land.

They cried on my shoulders and embraced me. "I have bought my ticket and my things are packed. I am going," I said.

4   For thirty days and nights the village people invited me to their houses, and I was dined and feted. It was hard not to change my mind and put off the trip. They came to see me off at the station. They waved their hands cheerfully though their eyes were sad. But my spirits were not dampened. I was looking ahead, thinking of your grandpa and San Francisco.

5   My brother went with me to Kobe, and not until the boat was pulling away from the pier did I feel a pain in my breast. Yes, I cried. The first night I could not sleep. I kept hearing my friends' words: "Hurry back. We will be waiting. Remember us. . . . Best of health to you." The boat began to toss and we could not go up on deck. I grew seasick. What kind of a boat? Tiny, though at that time we thought it was big. The liners of today are three and four times as large. . . . Yes, your grandma is old. She is of the first generation. You children are of the third. . . .

6   The sea was rough and I was sick almost all the way. There were others in the room just as ill. I couldn't touch the food. I began to have crazy thoughts. Why was I going to America? Why had I been foolish enough to leave my village? For days I could not lift my head. Turn back? Did the ship turn back for me? No, child. A steamer never turns back for an individual. Not for death or birth or storm. No more does life.

7   Now your grandma is old. She will die some day just like your grandpa. Yes, child, I know, you love me. But when I pass away and the days roll by, you will find life goes on. How do I know? Just this morning Annabelle lost a quarter somewhere on the street. Her mama told her not to hold it in her hands but put it in her purse. No, she wanted her way and lost it. That is experience, child. That is how I know. I lost Grandpa. I lost my boy. I lost my mother and father. Long ago I lost my friends in Japan. . . . Here, I am rambling. . . .

8   When the boat finally passed the Golden Gate, I had my first glimpse of San Francisco. I was on deck for hours, waiting for the golden city of dreams. I stood there with the other immigrants, chatting nervously and excitedly. First we saw only a thin shoreline. "America! America! We're in America!" someone cried. Others took up the cry, and presently the deck was full of eager faces. Finally we began to see the dirty brown hills and the houses that jutted out of the ground. This was different from what I had dreamed, and I was speechless. I had expected to see the green hills of Japan and the low sloping houses duplicated here. No, child, it wasn't disappointment exactly, but I had a lump in my throat. "This is San Francisco. My San Francisco," I murmured to myself.

9   What was I wearing, Annabelle? My best kimono, a beautiful thing. But do you know what your grandpa did when he saw me come off the boat? He looked at it and shook his head. He hauled me around as if he were ashamed of me. I could not understand.

10   "Never wear this thing again," he told me that night.

"Why?" I demanded. "It is a beautiful kimono."

"You look like a foreigner," he said. "You must dress like an American. You belong here."

11   He gave me a dress, a coat, a hat, stockings, and shoes, my first American clothes. I stopped dozens of times in front of the mirror to see how I looked. Yes, I remember the big hats they used to wear then, and the long skirts that dusted the dirt off the streets. Some day I shall go up to the attic of our Oakland home and bring down the album and show you the pictures of those old days.

12   I cannot find the street now where your grandpa and I lived that first year but it is somewhere in San Francisco. We had a small empty house and no money. We spread our blankets on the floor and slept. We used big boxes for tables and small ones for chairs. The city of my dreams began to frighten me. Rocks were thrown at the house and the windows smashed to bits. Loud cries and laughter followed each attack, and I cowered in the corner waiting for the end.

13   "Oh, why did I come? Whatever did we come for?" I asked your grandpa.

He only looked at me. "Just a little more time. . . . a little more time," his eyes seemed to say.

14   I could not refuse. But we moved out of San Francisco. We came across the Bay, and after much saving your grandpa bought a bathhouse in Oakland. And that was where your daddy was born. We lived in the rear, and for four years it was our home. Ah, the year your daddy was born! That was when for the first time I began to feel at home.

15   It was on account of a little neighbor, the white American wife of a Japanese acrobat. They were touring the country as headliners but had settled down in Oakland for some reason. They lived next door with their adopted Japanese children. "Mich-chan, Taka-chan! Come home! Mich-chan, Taka-chan!" Her cries used to ring across the yard like a caress.

16   The Japanese acrobat came often. "Please come and talk with my American wife. She is lonely and has no friend here," he told me.

17   I shook my head ashamedly. "I am lonely, too, but I cannot speak English. When your American wife starts talking, I am in trouble," I explained.

18   Then he would laugh and scold me. "Talk? You don't have to talk. My wife will understand. Please do not be afraid."

19   One day the American lady came, and we had tea. We drank silently and smiled. All the time I was hoping she would not begin talking. She liked my tea and cakes, I could tell. She talked of simple things so that I would grasp a little of it. She would pick up her teacup and ask, "Satsuma? Satsuma, Japan?"

20   I would nod eagerly. "Yes, Satsuma."

21   She came often. Every time we sat silently, sipped tea, and smiled. Every once in awhile her Japanese husband came and thanked me. "She is happy. She has a friend."

22   "I do not speak to her. I cannot express myself," I told him.

"No, no. She understands. You do not have to talk."

23   Ah, I can never forget her. She knitted baby clothes for your daddy. "I think it will be a girl," she said. But it was your daddy. I cried when she had to go away again. Yes, it was long ago. All your uncles and aunts came afterwards: Mamoru, Yuri, Willie, Mary Ann, Yoshio and Betty.

24   Yes, time is your friend in America, children. See, my face and hands are wrinkled, my hair gray. My teeth are gone, my figure bent. These are of America. I still cannot speak English too well, but I live among all kinds of people and come and go like the seasons, the bees, and the flowers. Ah, San Francisco, my dream city. My San Francisco is everywhere. I like the dirty brown hills, the black soil and the sandy beaches. I like the tall buildings, the bridges, the parks and the roar of city traffic. They are of me and I feel like humming.

25   You don't understand, Johnny? Ah, you are young. You will. Your grandma wants to be buried here in America. Yes, little ones. Once I had a brother and a sister in Japan. Long ago they wrote me a letter. Come back, sister, they said. We want to see you again. Hurry. Oh, it was long before you were born. But I did not return. I never saw them again. Now they are dead. I stayed in America; I belong here.

26   Now I do not ask myself: why did I come? The fog has lifted. Yes, Annabelle and Johnny, we are at war. I do not forget the fact. How can I ever forget? My mother country and my adopted land at war! Incredulous! After all these years when men of peace got along together. Your grandma sometimes cries in the night when her eyes open. No, not for herself. She is thinking of your Uncle Mamoru in the U.S. Infantry "somewhere" overseas and his comrades, and the people going through hardships and sufferings. In time of war, weak men fall and the strong triumph.

27   You will learn, little ones, that life is harsh at times. War is painful. If there were no war we would not be in a relocation center. We would be back in our house on Market Street, hanging out our wash on the clothesline and watering our flower garden. You would be attending school with your neighborhood friends. Ah, war is terrifying. It upsets personal life and hopes. But war has its good points too.

28   In what way, Johnny? Well, you learn your lessons quickly during wartimes. You become positive. You cannot sit on the fence, you must choose sides. War has given your grandmother an opportunity to find where her heart lay. To her surprise her choice had been made long ago, and no war will sway her a bit. For grandma the sky is clear. The sun is shining.

29   But I am old. This is where you come in. Children, you must grow big and useful. This is your world. . . .

30   Now run along to bed like a good boy and girl. Sleep and rise early. Tomorrow is coming, children.

SLANT-EYED AMERICANS

1 My mother was commenting on the fine California weather. It was Sunday noon, December 7. We were having our lunch, and I had the radio going. "Let's take the afternoon off and go to the city," I said to Mother.

2 "All right. We shall go," she said dreamily. "Ah, four months ago my boy left Hayward to join the army, and a fine send-off he had. Our good friends—ah, I shall never forget the day of his departure."

3 "We'll visit some of our friends in Oakland and then take in a movie," I said. "Care to come along, Papa?"

Father shook his head. "No, I'll stay home and take it easy."

"That's his heaven," Mother commented. "To stay home, read the papers over and over, and smoke his Bull Durham."

4 I laughed. Suddenly the musical program was cut off as a special announcement came over the air: At 7:25 a.m. this morning a squadron of Japanese bombing planes attacked Pearl Harbor. The battle is still in progress.

5 "What's this? Listen to the announcement," I cried, going to the radio.

6 Abruptly the announcement stopped and the musicale continued.

7 "What is it?" Mother asked. "What has happened?"

"The radio reports that the Japanese planes attacked Hawaii this morning," I said incredulously. "It couldn't be true."

"It must be a mistake. Couldn't it have been a part of a play?" asked Mother.

8 I dialed other stations. Several minutes later one of the stations confirmed the bulletin.

"It must be true," Father said quietly.

I said, "Japan has declared war on the United States and Great Britain."

9 The room became quiet but for the special bulletin coming in every now and then.

10 "It cannot be true, yet it must be so," Father said over and over.

"Can it be one of those programs scaring the people about invasion?" Mother asked me.

"No, I'm sure this is a news report," I replied.

11 Mother's last ray of hope paled and her eyes became dull. "Why did it have to happen? The common people in Japan don't want war, and we don't want war. Here the people are peace-loving. Why cannot the peoples of the earth live together peacefully?"

12 "Since Japan declared war on the United States it'll mean that you parents of American citizens have become enemy aliens," I said.

"Enemy aliens," my mother whispered.

13 Night came but sleep did not come. We sat up late in the night hoping against hope that some good news would come, retracting the news of vicious attack and open hostilities.

14 "This is very bad for the people with Japanese faces," I said.

Father slowly shook his head.

"What shall we do?" asked Mother.

"What can we do?" Father said helplessly.

15   At the flower market next morning the growers were present but the buyers were scarce. The place looked empty and deserted. "Our business is shot to pieces," one of the boys said.

16   "Who'll buy flowers now?" another called.

Don Haley, the seedsman, came over looking bewildered. "I suppose you don't need seeds now."

We shook our heads.

"It looks bad," I said. "Will it affect your business?"

"Flower seed sale will drop but the vegetable seeds will move quicker," Don said. "I think I'll have to put more time on the vegetable seeds."

17   Nobu Hiramatsu who had been thinking of building another greenhouse joined us. He had plans to grow more carnations and expand his business.

"What's going to happen to your plans, Nobu?" asked one of the boys.

"Nothing. I'm going to sit tight and see how the things turn out," he said.

"Flowers and war don't go together," Don said. "You cannot concentrate too much on beauty when destruction is going about you."

"Sure, pretty soon we'll raise vegetables instead of flowers," Grasselli said.

18   A moment later the market opened and we went back to the tables to sell our flowers. Several buyers came in and purchased a little. The flowers didn't move at all. Just as I was about to leave the place I met Tom Yamashita, the Nisei gardener with a future.

19   "What are you doing here, Tom? What's the matter with your work?" I asked as a I noticed his pale face.

"I was too sick with yesterday's news so I didn't work," he said. "This is the end. I am done for."

"No, you're not. Buck up, Tom," I cried. "You have a good future, don't lose hope."

"Sometimes I feel all right. You are an American, I tell myself. Devote your energy and life to the American way of life. Long before this my mind was made up to become a true American. This morning my Caucasian American friends sympathized with me. I felt good and was grateful. Our opportunity has come to express ourselves and act. We are Americans in thought and action. I felt like leaping to work. Then I got sick again because I got to thinking that Japan was the country that attacked the United States. I wanted to bury myself for shame."

20   I put my hand on his shoulder. "We all feel the same way, Tom. We're human so we flounder around awhile when an unexpected and big problem confronts us, but now that situation has to be passed by. We can't live in the same stage long. We have to move along, face the reality no matter what's in store for us."

21   Tom stood silently.

22   "Let's go to my house and take the afternoon off," I suggested. "We'll face a new world tomorrow morning with boldness and strength. What do you say, Tom?"

"All right," Tom agreed.

23   At home Mother was anxiously waiting for me. When she saw Tom with me her eyes brightened. Tom Yamashita was a favorite of my mother's.

24   "Look, a telegram from Kazuo!" she cried to me, holding up an envelope. "Read it and tell me what he says."

25   I tore it open and read. "He wants us to send $45 for train fare. He has a good chance for a furlough."

26   Mother fairly leaped in the air with the news. She had not seen my brother for four months. "How wonderful! This can happen only in America."

27   Suddenly she noticed Tom looking glum, and pushed him in the house. "Cheer up, Tom. This is no time for young folks to despair. Roll up your sleeves and get to work. America needs you."

28   Tom smiled for the first time and looked at me.

29   "See, Tom?" I said. "She's quick to recover. Yesterday she was wilted, and she's seventy-three."

"Tom, did you go to your gardens today?" she asked him.

"No."

"Why not?" she asked, and then added quickly. "You young men should work hard all the more, keeping up the normal routine of life. You ought to know, Tom, that if everybody dropped their work everything would go to seed. Who's going to take care of the gardens if you won't?"

30   Tom kept still.

31   Mother poured tea and brought the cookies. "Don't worry about your old folks. We have stayed here to belong to the American way of life. Time will tell our true purpose. We remained in America for permanence—not for temporary convenience. We common people need not fear."

32   "I guess you are right," Tom agreed.

"And America is right. She cannot fail. Her principles will stand the test of time and tyranny. Someday agression will be outlawed by all nations."

33   Mother left the room to prepare the dinner. Tom got up and began to walk up and down the room. Several times he looked out the window and watched the wind blow over the field.

34   "Yes, if the gardens are ruined I'll rebuild them," he said. "I'll take charge of every garden in the city. All the gardens of America for that matter. I'll rebuild them as fast as the enemies wreck them. We'll have nature on our side and you cannot crush nature."

35   I smiled and nodded. "Good for you! Tomorrow we'll get up early in the morning and work, sweat, and create. Let's shake on it."

36   We solemnly shook hands, and by the grip of his fingers I knew he was ready to lay down his life for America and for his gardens.

37 "No word from him yet," Mother said worriedly. "He should have arrived yesterday. What's happened to him?"

38 It was eight in the evening, and we had had no word from my brother
for several days.

39 "He's not coming home tonight. It's too late now," I said. "He should
have arrived in Oakland this morning at the latest."

40 Our work had piled up and we had to work late into the night. There
were still some pompons to bunch. Faintly the phone rang in the house.

41 "The phone!" cried Mother excitedly. "It's Kazuo, sure enough."

42 In the flurry of several minutes I answered the phone, greeted my
brother, and was on my way to San Leandro to drive him home. On the
way I tried to think of the many things I wanted to say. From the moment I
spotted him waiting on the corner I could not say the thing I wanted to. I
took his bag and he got in the car, and for some time we did not say anything. Then I asked him how the weather had been in Texas and how he
had been.

43 "We were waiting for you since yesterday," I said. "Mother is home getting the supper ready. You haven't eaten yet, have you?"

He shook his head. "The train was late getting into Los Angeles. We were
eight hours behind time and I should have reached San Francisco this
morning around eight."

44 Reaching home it was the same way. Mother could not say anything.
"We have nothing special tonight, wish we had something good."

45 "Anything would do, Mama," my brother said.

46 Father sat in the room reading the papers but his eyes were over the
sheet and his hands were trembling. Mother scurried about getting his
supper ready. I sat across the table from my brother, and in the silence
which was action I watched the wave of emotions in the room. My brother
was aware of it too. He sat there without a word, but I knew he understood. Not many years ago he was the baby of the family, having never
been away from home. Now he was on his own, his quiet confidence actually making him appear larger. Keep up the fire, that was his company's
motto. It was evident that he was a soldier. He had gone beyond life and
death matters, where the true soldiers of war or peace must travel, and
had returned.

47 For five short days we went about our daily task, picking and bunch-
ing the flowers of Christmas, eating heavy meals, and visiting the inti-
mates. It was as if we were waiting for the hour of his departure, the time
being so short. Every minute was crowded with privacy, friends, and
nursery work. Too soon the time for his train came but the family had little to talk.

48 "Kazuo, don't worry about home or me," Mother said as we rode into
town.

"Take care of yourself," my brother told her.

49   At the 16th Street Station Mother's close friend was waiting for us. She came to bid my brother goodbye. We had fifteen minutes to wait. My brother bought a copy of *The Coast* to see if his cartoons were in.

50   "Are you in this month's issue?" I asked.

"I haven't seen it yet," he said, leafing the pages. "Yes, I'm in. Here it is."

"Good!" I said. "Keep trying hard. Someday peace will come, and when you return laughter will reign once again."

51   My mother showed his cartoon to her friend. The train came in and we got up. It was a long one. We rushed to the Los Angeles-bound coach.

52   Mother's friend shook hands with my brother. "Give your best to America. Our people's honor depends on you Nisei soldiers."

53   My brother nodded and then glanced at Mother. For a moment her eyes twinkled and she nodded. He waved good-bye from the platform. Once inside the train we lost him. When the train began to move my mother cried, "Why doesn't he pull up the shades and look out? Others are doing it."

54   We stood and watched until the last of the train was lost in the night of darkness.

from Mori, Toshio. *Yokohama, California*. Seattle: University of Washington Press, 1985 (1949 by Caxton Printers, Ltd., Caxton, Idaho.).

♦ Understanding Each Other: Discussion Questions

1. What is life like in America for the narrator of this story? Are her reactions similar to or different from those of the participants in the scenario? How did you feel when you first arrived in the United States?

2. To whom is the narrator in *Yokohama, California* speaking? What are the children like? Are they similar to or different from the children in the scenario? Do they have the same questions? Do they have the same problems?

3. How did the narrator's friends and family react when she left her homeland to come to the United States? Did anything occur in the scenario to tell you how those participants felt about leaving their homeland? How did your family and friends react when you left to come to the United States?

4. List five *adjectives* which describe the narrator of *Yokohama, California*. Why do you think the author made his central character a woman? Do you know anyone from your country who came to the United States under the same circumstances as she did? Do these two people share any of the same characteristics?

5. What is the Japanese acrobat like? Do you know anyone in your hometown who has an American husband or wife, or a spouse from a different country? How do they feel living so far away from their own countries? Are their reactions the same as the acrobat's wife, or are they different? How do you feel, living or staying in America?

6. How does the narrator's husband react to her arriving in a kimono? What is your reaction to what he says to her? Do you agree or disagree with his point of view? Did a similar point of view come up in the scenario?
7. What kinds of events make the narrator feel at home in America? What kinds of things make you feel at ease in the United States?
8. How does the narrator feel when her homeland and her new country go to war? Would you feel the same way, or would you feel different about it? What legacy does the narrator want her descendants to have? What legacy do you want for your children and grandchildren?
9. What effects on the mood in the Japanese American family occur as the result of being labeled "enemy aliens"?

◆ Interactive Grammar and Usage: Rules in Reflection

Working with another student, practice standard English usage by filling in the blanks below. Your teacher may give you a list of choices. Your goal is to make the passage both coherent and cohesive. After filling in all the blanks, go back and reread the passage, making any changes in the words selected to improve its internal cohesiveness. Some of the choices are those found in the reading; others are close in meaning. Be prepared to explain the reasons for your choices. Then formulate the rules of grammar and usage which are implicit here. The first sentence is done for you.

In <u>the</u> flurry of several minutes I <u>answered</u> the phone, <u>greeted</u> my brother, <u>and</u> was on my way <u>to</u> San Leandro to drive him home. _____1 the way _____2 tried to think of the many _____3 I wanted to say. From the moment I _____4 him waiting _____5 the corner I could not say the thing _____6 wanted to. I took his bag and he _____7 in the car, and for _____8 time we did _____9 say anything. _____10 I asked _____11 how the weather _____12 been _____13 Texas and _____14 he had _____15.

"_____16 _____17 waiting _____18 you _____19 yesterday," I said. "Mother is _____20 getting _____21 supper ready. You _____22 eaten _____23, _____24 _____25?"

♦ Increasing Word Power: Vocabulary In Context

Working with a partner, decide on the meaning *in context* of each of the following words or phrases. Then look up each item in a good English-English dictionary. Does the context meaning of the word in the reading differ in any way from the dictionary's definition? If so, how did the context help you understand the meaning of the word as used in the passage?

Word	Meaning in This Context	Dictionary Definition
shocked		
enticing		
coins		
mid-Pacific		
determined		
embraced		
feted		
dampened		
pier		
glimpse		
chatting		
jutted		
sloping		
disappointment		
ashamed		

Word	Meaning in This Context	Dictionary Definition
attic		
acrobat		
headliners		
lonely		
wrinkled		
buried		
incredulous		
relocation center		
terrifying		
clothesline		
dreamily		
Bull Durham		
squadron		
musicale		
dialed		
aliens		
vicious		
hostilities		
scarce		
carnations		
pale		
buck up		
flounder		
tyranny		
scurried		

◆ Finding Your Own Voice: For Discussion and Writing

1. With whom did you identify in this story? Why did you like that particular character? Were you moved by the narrator's experiences? What do you think will happen to the narrator's children and grandchildren?
2. Describe your own experiences and feelings about living in the United States.
3. What do you think about the relationship between husbands and wives today? How does that relationship compare with the one described in *Yokohama, California*? How are they similar or different? Do you have any explanation for *why* a change has occurred? You might write an essay on this subject.
4. Finish the narrator's story: tell what you think happens to her and to her brother.
5. Perform the scenario "School days" to bring your work with this chapter full circle. Then write an essay about one aspect of this scenario and bring it into class for the group to critique and polish.

CHAPTER 8

Middle-Eastern American

◆ Listening to Each Other: Scenario

See Chapter 1 for instructions on how to perform a scenario.
Prepare and perform the scenario "Curricular improvements."

◆ Speaking Out: Debriefing Questions

1. Have you ever served on a school board or on a committee that was responsible for school programs? How do such organizations work?
2. Which do you think is more important: a class in your native language or a new gymnasium? Explain why.
3. With which character in the scenario did you identify? Why do you empathize with that person?
4. If the scenario were acted out again, would you do or say anything different? Give your reasons for the changes.
5. How important do you think it is for immigrants to have positive feelings about their background?

◆ Reaching Out: Suggestions for Further Activities

1. School-board meetings in the United States are open to the public. Arrange to attend a local meeting. What kinds of things do board members discuss?

2. Write a scenario for the class that is based on the needs of your school, and hold a mock board meeting. What are some of the important issues that you want to make sure are discussed? If those issues are not particularly important to others, what will you do to have them considered by the group?

3. Have a class discussion in which you and your classmates compare the ways that schools are run in your native countries. Are there school boards, for example?

4. In the United States there is an organization called the Parent Teacher Association (PTA), which is very vocal in public-school affairs. Have you ever attended a PTA meeting? If so, describe what happened during the meeting. Did you feel welcome? If you have never been to such a meeting, arrange to go, as a class if possible.

5. Write an essay about one aspect of the scenario and bring it into class for the group to critique and polish.

◆ Reading: From *Syrian Yankee*, by Salom Rizk

Read the following selection, keeping in mind the scenario you have already experienced. It is always a good idea to have an English-English dictionary at hand when you read. A useful technique is to read the selection through quickly the first time, highlighting words or phrases that you think you need to look up. Then go back and do a more careful reading, looking up unfamiliar words.

1   It was decided to start me out in the fourth grade. Imagine how I felt, a grown man in long pants going to school with a bunch of kids, little boys in knee breeches and little girls in short frocks. When the full force of this discrepancy struck me, I knew I was not going to like school. I expected the youngsters to make fun of me, to laugh at my ignorance, my backwardness, and my awful accent. Strangely, nothing of the kind happened. Sometimes they would laugh at the way I scrambled the language, but it was not in ridicule. It was all in good hearty fun which I enjoyed as much as they did.

2   Both my teachers and my little classmates were exceedingly helpful. My eagerness to learn the English language was equaled by the enthusiasm of my teachers to help me. I was like a child learning his first words, and they almost applauded me every time I acquired a new word or turned a new sentence. My progress seemed to give them endless pleasure, and this spurred me on to extra effort.

3   By applying myself in my spare time and through special tutoring from my teachers I was able to move ahead rapidly. Every few weeks came a promotion until, by the end of the semester, I was ready for ninth-grade English.

4   I hadn't worked long on the English language, however, before I was convinced I could not depend on logic to learn it. I thought at first it would be something like my native tongue, that if you learned the letters of the alphabet and their sounds, plus some rules of grammar and spelling, you could learn by yourself.

5   But I had not counted on the English language being so unreasonable. There was, for example, a whole mess of sounds which were not represented in the alphabet. So it seemed somebody had gone to the trouble to juggle the letters until they fell into the most astonishing combinations, *ch, sh, ph, gh* being only among the least unpronounceable cases. After struggling for hours with certain alphabetical monstrosities, I was convinced that no one without English ancestors could ever hope to discover their sounds. But even worse than all this, when there was a very obvious letter in the alphabet to stand for a sound, somebody had labored to invent combinations which defied all my attempts at pronunciation. It was my habit to hunt in the dictionary for new words to add to my vocabulary, and one day I came across a real freak: "phthisic." How do you pronounce that? *Phth?* I find there is a simple letter in the alphabet to stand for the sound this four-letter behemoth is supposed to make. It is the letter *t*, twenty letters down in the alphabet and not so hard to find, either. Yet here is this *phth*, a monument to Anglo-Saxon ingenuity—one sound, four letters, and you have to guess which one to pronounce. I used to puzzle no end over words like "freight" and "weight," and I don't understand yet why the word "colonel" is mispronounced so badly. Many times I would despair of either learning or reforming a language which behaved so unreasonably.

6   And then I had to memorize a whole chaos of vowel sounds, long *a*, short *a*, broad *a*, etc., etc., etc. The letter *a*, in fact, was the worst offender, the black sheep in the vowel family. And a close second was his fat brother, the letter *o*, with six different noises to his credit. The letter *e* with a little less criminal talent has only five, yet it could be at times as wicked as the worst. But the letter *i*—I have a special affection for the letter *i*. It comes the nearest to being a second cousin of the Syrian vowels of any letter in the English alphabet. It has only two sounds and does not require you to take signing lessons before you can hit them.

7   Pronouns used to give me a lot of trouble, too. I would puzzle over them a whole evening. They behaved with no more respect for law and order than the vowels or those distressing consonant combinations. It seemed to me that if it is right to say "he," "his," "him," why shouldn't it follow: "she," "shis," "shim"? But no. The pundits had to make it "she," "her," and "hers" and complicate the whole business of the immigrant trying to become a good American.

8   All these peculiarities made it infinitely harder for me to learn the language, and sometimes I was indignant with the anonymous fathers of a tongue which I would not learn by myself. I had to wait for my teacher or some friend to help me pronounce almost every single word.

9   I asked one of my teachers about all this.

"Are there no rules to the English language?"

"Yes, most certainly, there are rules," she assured me, "but there are exceptions to the rules."

10   But that did not seem to explain the difficulty. Later the real explanation came out: there were not only exceptions to the rules, but exceptions to the exceptions.

11   I was particularly bothered by the exceptions to the forming of plurals. I was told that the plural of any word was made by adding *s* or *es*, but when I made "foot" into "foots," I learned that was wrong. It was "feet," just as the plural of "tooth" is "teeth." Well, I had discovered a new rule. But when I made the word "booth" into "beeth," my teachers said the old rule applied and it was "booths." By this time my mind was so full of confusion that I was almost in a mood to stick to my native Syrian.

12   I went on to learn to my astonishment that "mouse" does not become "mouses" the way "house" becomes "houses" and that it is never right to say "hice" for the plural of "house" the way you say "mice" for the plural of "mouse" or "lice" for the plural of "louse." But how was I supposed to tell? The plural of "sheep" is neither "sheeps" nor "shoop," but "sheep," just like the singular, right straight through to ten million or even a billion billion of them. But a "baby beef" in the herd is not "baby beef" or "baby beefs" or "baby boofs," but "baby beeves." They told me that "ox" does not become "oxes" as "box" becomes "boxes." Then, when I thought I had found a clue, namely, that live things form different plurals from inanimate things, and proceeded to make "foxen" out of "fox," the teachers told me I was wrong again. They said it was "foxes." What was I to do? I was ready to appeal to the legislature for a law and make it just plain "oxen" and "foxen" and "boxen."

13   At last there was nothing for me to do but to memorize all this and get used to it. But sometimes I revolted, especially when my ignorance of how to spell or pronounce the language brought me embarrassment.

14   One day I was ordering a meal in a restaurant. It was just before the repeal of prohibition. On the menu they had "spiced tomato juice." I had just learned that the letter *c* is sometimes pronounced hard, as in "cat." So after studying for a while I ordered "spiked tomato juice" and was icily informed that they did not serve liquor there.

15   During this first year in school came one of my greatest astonishments: that Americans—especially young school-going Americans—took their many blessings and opportunities so much for granted. That everybody could speak and write and worship as he pleased did not seem strange to anybody. That education was free for everyone down to the humblest of citizens amazed no one. In Ain Arab I used to long for just one sheet of paper to write on. I hungered for just one book to read, one book to call my own, and I used to rescue scraps of Syrian newspaper from the gutters of Beirut, take them home, and feast on them a whole evening. But here in America books and papers were everywhere, the schools were as magnifi-

cent as palaces and the equipment comfortable, stimulating, breath-taking. I was fascinated by all the richness, the maps and pictures on the walls, the great blackboards, all the high windows, and the many lights which were turned on when it was cloudy outdoors. How could anyone take all this grand achievement for granted?

16   I saw these precious privileges and opportunities wasted by too many young Americans who evidently could not comprehend what my experience had forced upon me: the difference, the unbelievable contrast, between that old world their forefathers had left and this new world they had built. I saw youngsters actually despising the school and what it stood for, showing contempt for those who were brighter or studied harder than they did. I saw them playing hooky, pretending sickness, "getting by" with as little learning as possible. Some of them boasted of their skill in cheating and laughed up their sleeves at their unwitting teachers. They disfigured the beautiful surroundings lavished upon them, carving their initials on the furniture and marking up the walls.

17   I could not understand at first how anyone could be so heedless, so negligent, and even contemptuous of these hard-won common possessions. I learned how the ancestors of these students had worked and fought and sacrificed for the rights they took so much for granted. The more I dug into American history, reading much of it in the Syrian language, the greater became my astonishment. I felt that I ought to do something to awaken my fellow Americans to all these blessings. I now had a new, powerful incentive to learn the language of the country of which I was fortunate enough to be a citizen.

18   Strangely, I did not recognize my first opportunity to discuss appreciation of American democracy, and only gradually did it dawn upon me that I had found the avenue which was to become a career for me. It happened this way. One day the teacher asked the class to write a theme.

19   "But I cannot write," I told her.
      "You can talk, though, can't you, Sam?" she said, smiling at me.
      "Yes, I can talk—a little, but I can't write themes."
      "Suppose that, instead of writing a theme, you tell us your story."
      "Tell my story?"
      "Yes, tell us something about yourself, your life in Syria, how you found out you were an American, your struggles to reach this country, and how you feel about things. You don't have to make it long, and I know it will be interesting to all of us."

20   The more I thought of that assignment, the more it terrified me. I had never stood before an audience in my life. I had told my teacher that my talk would be lousy, and I was sure it would. I looked forward to the ordeal with the same misgivings which torment a soldier the first time he goes into the firing line.

21   Four days later I stood before nearly forty youngsters. My knees promptly became as weak as jelly, my tongue as heavy as a mountain, my throat dry. My hands felt as big as those packing-house hams. After an

eternity of silence, during which I adjusted my hands and feet in all the awkward positions I could think of, my tongue came free and I began to use it. The first thing I said was, "Hello!" Everybody laughed.

22   Twenty-five minutes later I sat down, hardly aware of the time that had passed. The youngsters were clamoring for more. But the ordeal was over. I had not imagined that anyone could forget himself so completely. Speaking and sleeping have at least one thing in common: when you get through you don't know just how long you've been at them.

23   Of course I was pleased by this success, even though it was only with forty school kids. But I knew it was not due to my skill with the language. It was the power of the story itself. Anybody else living through the same experience could have done as well, probably better.

24   Within the next few weeks I addressed nearly all the classes in the school. My teacher told the other teachers, and they invited me to repeat my story to their pupils. With each telling my confidence mounted. Each time I tried to use a wider range of words, tried to get the feel of phrases which would mean the most to the youngsters. All these opportunities to speak were a great encouragement to me and gave my tussles with the English language extra motive and determination. When the teachers began to tell me how they were awakened to a new appreciation of their American blessings, I began to see my story as the answer to this growing desire within me.

25   The next semester I was taking high-school English. One day the speech teacher said to me:

"Sam, wouldn't you like to take part in some extracurricular activity?"

"Extracurricular?" I said, puzzled, wrapping my tongue around the word as best I could.

"Yes, something besides your regular English studies, something like Gymnasium, Dramatics, or Glee Club."

"What do you think I could do best?" I asked.

"Here is a list of activities. Why don't you look them over and check the one you want?"

26   I studied the list, wondering what it was all about, finally making a mark after "Glee Club."

"Do you know what Glee Club is?"

"No, but I'll try anything once."

"Glee Club is singing, and really, Sam, I don't think you'll make much of a singer."

"No, I'm a lousy singer. Maybe you give me something where I speak—or learn speaking better."

"Sam, why don't you try oratory? We have a high-school contest in oratory, and I think I can find an oration that will suit you just fine."

27   So I found out what an oration was. They gave me one to memorize entitled "The Immigrant Speaks." I didn't know the meaning of all the words, and learning to pronounce them was like memorizing nonsense. But I

worked hard at it. Wherever the teacher said to lift my voice, I lifted it; wherever to lower it, I lowered it. Wherever she said to put a gesture, I put it. It was all as mechanical as operating an automobile, a push-button performance, but the teacher said it was good, especially the sincerity. Well, I was beginning to understand a little of what I was saying.

28   The night of the local contest I took the bus down to the school, delivered "The Immigrant Speaks" to a large audience, and returned immediately to the restaurant to scrub floors.

29   About ten-thirty the telephone rang.

"Hello, is this Sam Rizk?" a woman's voice asked.

"Yes, this is Sam Rizk."

"Sam, congratulations. You won."

"I one?"

"Yes, you won. Isn't that wonderful?"

"I one? Sure I one. I am not two."

"No, no, Sam. This is Mrs. Gaunt. You have first place in the speaking contest."

30   So I had first place! I one. This English language had a little logic to it after all. When you count, the first number is one. If you get in a contest, you one. It was onederful. Maybe I would be an American yet, a real American speaking English like other Americans.

31   But soon I was to suffer a blow to this slender hope. In the district oratorical contest, I lost. The judges said the oration was fine, sincere, forceful, impressive, well delivered, but alas, they said, "The Immigrant Speaks" with an accent.

from *Syrian Yankee* by Salom Rizk, copyright 1943 by Salom Rizk. Used by permission of Doubleday, a division of Bantam Doubleday Dell Publishing Group, Inc.

♦ Understanding Each Other: Discussion Questions

1. Have you ever felt like Sam (Salom Rizk), or been in a situation like his, studying a language alongside students much younger than yourself?

2. What are *extracurricular activities*? List some of the possibilities which Rizk had the opportunity to choose from. What extracurricular activities do you have at your school? Are there many more now, compared to in Sam's day? Do you participate in these activities?

3. How long is a public-school semester in most American schools? In your country's public schools? At what level does Sam begin studying English? After one semester, what level has he reached?

4. What frustrations does Rizk have with the sounds and grammar of English? Have you experienced any of the same frustrations?

5. Rizk has used many American-English idioms and metaphors throughout his book. Find as many of these words and phrases as you can in this excerpt and be prepared to explain their meanings.

6. What does the phrase "the black sheep of the family" mean? How does Rizk paraphrase these words in describing his struggles with English?

7. Where does the phrase "law and order" (paragraph 7) come from? In paragraph 8, is the word *tongue* used to mean a part of the anatomy or something else?

8. What was *prohibition?* When was it in effect in the United States? Has your country ever had, or does it now have, such laws? What is "spiked" tomato juice?

9. During his first year of school, what kinds of things does Rizk observe American students doing that absolutely astonish him? Do you see any of these same things today? Do students in your home country behave like this?

10. What mission does Rizk take on which gives him a powerful incentive to learn English? What "avenue" does he find to fulfill this mission? What specific things does he do?

11. What happens to Sam in the district oratorical contest? What is ironic about the outcome?

12. What observations can you make about how well Rizk learned English? Take the breadth of his vocabulary and his knowledge of American idioms and metaphors into consideration in your analysis. Explain the pun "onederful" (in the next-to-the-last paragraph).

◆ Interactive Grammar and Usage: Rules in Reflection

Parallelism in English means not only a repeated structural pattern *within* a sentence but also a structural pattern repeated from *sentence to sentence*. Conferring with a partner, fill in the blanks below. Your teacher will give you a list of choices in class. Bear in mind that you can create coherence and cohesiveness by using parallel structures. When you have finished, generalize the syntactical rules implicit here. The first sentence is done for you.

During this first year in school came one of my greatest astonishments: that Americans—especially young school-going Americans—took their many blessings and opportunities so much for granted. _____ 1 could _____ 2 and _____ 3 as he pleased did not seem strange to anybody. _____ 4 was free for everyone down to the humblest of citizens amazed no one. In Ain Arab I used to _____ 5 just _____ 6 of paper _____ 7 . I hungered for _____ 8 one _____ 9 _____ 10 , _____ 11 _____ 12 my own, _____ 13 rescue scraps of Syrian newspaper from the gutters of Beirut, _____ 14 home, and _____ 15 a whole evening. But here in America _____ 16 were everywhere, the _____ 17 as magnificent as palaces and _____ 18 _____ 19 , stimulating, _____ 20 . I was fascinated by _____ 21 , the _____ 22 pictures on the walls, _____ 23 , all _____ 24 windows, _____ 25 which were turned on when it was cloudy outdoors. How could anyone take all this grand achievement for granted?

◆ *Syrian Yankee* Grammar and Usage Choice List

all the equipment	books and papers
all the poverty	book and paper
all the richness	breath-taking
and I used to	buildings were
and they used to	but the many lights
and the many lights	carry them
book	comfortable

dull
feast on them
for the equipment
gyms were
horrifying
just
long for
maps and
one book
one sheet
paper
say
schools and school children
schools were
several sheets
speak
stupendous

take them
That education
That everybody
That I
That student
the broken
the equipment
the great blackboards
the graffiti
the high
the stained glass
to call
took them
to read
to write on
trying to
write and worship

♦ Increasing Word Power: Vocabulary in Context

Working with a partner, decide on the meaning *in context* of each of the following words or phrases. Then look up each item in a good English-English dictionary. Does the context meaning of the word in the reading differ in any way from the dictionary's definition? If so, how did the context help you understand the meaning of the word as used in the passage?

Word	Meaning in This Context	Dictionary Definition
knee breeches		
frocks		
discrepancy		
hearty		
spur on		
be convinced		
logic		
juggle		
monstrosities		
defied		
phthisic		
behemoth		
puzzle		
pundits		
indignant		
stick to		
inanimate		

Word	Meaning in This Context	Dictionary Definition
icily		
gutters		
feast on		
be fascinated by		
take for granted		
playing hooky		
laugh up one's sleeve		
lavished		
carve		
negligent		
hard-won		
dig into		
lousy		
misgivings		
torment		
as weak as jelly		
packing house		
eternity		
clamor for		
tussles		
nonsense		
scrub		
suffer a blow		

◆ Finding Your Own Voice: For Discussion and Writing

1. Write a ten-minute speech on an important subject and hold an oratorical contest in your class. If your school already has an oratorical society, ask your teacher to invite them to visit your class to give an exhibition of oratorical skills before your contest is held. Discuss the hallmarks of a good speaker.
2. Try to attend a public lecture; if possible, go with other members of your class. Take notes on *how* the lecture was presented. Afterwards, discuss what was presented and what made the talk effective or ineffective.
3. Write a story or an essay dealing with your own tussles with English.
4. Write a story or an essay about the struggles an acquaintance had learning English. Include illustrations and details to bring your description to life.
5. Perform the scenario "Playing John Alden" to bring your work with this chapter full circle. Your teacher may ask you to write an essay about the theme of this scenario, by yourself or as part of a group.

CHAPTER 9

Native-American

◆ Listening to Each Other: Scenario

See Chapter 1 for instructions on how to perform a scenario.
   Prepare and perform the scenario "A sense of humor."

◆ Speaking Out: Debriefing Questions

1. How did the two friends in the scenario solve the dilemma? Were they able to resolve it so that each of them "won"?
2. What are some ways to find out about humorous things in other cultures?
3. How could you let someone know in a diplomatic way that a joke he or she told was inappropriate?
4. What subjects in the United States do Americans joke about? What subjects are taboo?
5. What kinds of jokes are appropriate in your native culture? Are any subjects taboo?

◆ Reaching Out: Suggestions for Further Activities

1. Read an autobiography of a famous Indian chief such as Sitting Bull, Tecumseh, or Cochise; or read about Sacagawea, a famous guide. Pre-

pare that person's story and present it from the first-person point of view to the class.

2. Before immigrants from Europe and Asia began to settle the United States, millions of Native-Americans inhabited the entire territory. Many states have Indian reservations today, and most have a museum of natural history which displays scenes and artifacts from tribal life. If possible, visit the nearest reservation and talk with some Native-Americans, to try to understand their feelings, or attend an Indian tribal powwow. You might also see an American Indian dance company perform. There are films and videos available on these subjects that you can view if it is not possible for you to visit a reservation or attend a performance in person.

3. A Hollywood film which shows Native-American humor is *Little Big Man* (with Dustin Hoffman). If possible, view this film and take notes on Indian culture and history. Then, after reading the excerpt which follows, compare the film account with Deloria's account of Indian life. Other films, such as *Tell Them Willie Boy Was Here* (starring Robert Redford), *Cheyenne Autumn* (with Richard Widmark), and *Dances with Wolves* (starring Kevin Costner), which present truthful but very somber accounts of Indian life, are also worth seeing.

◆ Reading: From *Custer Died for Your Sins*, by Vine Deloria, Jr.

Read the following selection, keeping in mind the scenario you have already experienced. It is always a good idea to have an English-English dictionary at hand when you read. A useful technique is to read the selection through quickly the first time, highlighting words or phrases that you think you need to look up. Then go back and do a more careful reading, looking up unfamiliar words.

INDIAN HUMOR

1   One of the best ways to understand a people is to know what makes them laugh. Laughter encompasses the limits of the soul. In humor life is redefined and accepted. Irony and satire provide much keener insights into a group's collective psyche and values than do years of research.

It has always been a great disappointment to Indian people that the humorous side of Indian life has not been mentioned by professed experts on Indian Affairs. Rather the image of the granite-faced grunting redskin has been perpetuated by American mythology . . .

2   The Indian people are exactly opposite of the popular stereotype. I sometimes wonder how anything is accomplished by Indians because of

the apparent overemphasis on humor within the Indian world. Indians have found a humorous side of nearly every problem and the experiences of life have generally been so well defined through jokes and stories that they have become a thing in themselves . . . .

3 The early reservation days were times when humorous incidents abounded as Indians tried to adapt to the strange new white ways and occasionally found themselves in great dilemmas.

4 At Fort Sisseton, in Dakota territory, Indians were encouraged to enlist as scouts for the Army after the Minnesota Wars. Among the requirements for enlistment were a working knowledge of English and having attained twenty-one years of age. But these requirements were rarely met. Scouts were scarce and the goal was to keep a company of scouts at full strength, not to follow regulations from Washington to the letter.

5 In a short time the Army had a company of scouts who were very efficient but didn't know enough English to understand a complete sentence. Washington, finding out about the situation, as bureaucracies occasionally do, sent an inspector to check on the situation. While he was en route, orders to disband the scouts arrived, and so his task became one of closing the unit and making the mustering-out payments.

6 The scouts had lined up outside the command officer's quarters and were interviewed one by one. They were given their choice of taking money, horses, or a combination of the two as their final severance pay from the Army. Those who could not speak English were severely reprimanded and tended to get poorer horses in payment because of their obvious disregard of the regulations.

7 One young scout, who was obviously in violation of both requirements, was very worried about his interview. He quizzed the scouts who came from the room about the interview. To a man they repeated the same story: "You will be asked three questions, how old you are, how long you have been with the scouts, and whether you want money or horses for your mustering-out pay."

8 The young scout memorized the appropriate answers and prepared himself for his turn with the inspector. When his turn came he entered the room, scared to death but determined to do his best. He stood at attention before the man from Washington, eager to give his answers and get out of there.

9 The inspector, tired after a number of interviews, wearily looked up and inquired:

"How long have you been in the scouts?"

"Twenty years," the Indian replied with a grin.

10 The inspector stopped short and looked at the young man. Here was a man who looked only eighteen or twenty, yet he had served some twenty years in the scouts. He must have been one of the earliest recruits. It just

didn't seem possible. Yet, the inspector thought, you can't tell an Indian's age from the way he looks, they sure can fool you sometimes. Or was he losing his mind after interviewing so many people in so short a time? Perhaps it was the Dakota heat. At any rate, he continued the interview.

"How old are you?" he continued.

"Three years."

A look of shock rippled across the inspector's face. Could this be some mysterious Indian way of keeping time? Or was he now delirious?

"Am I crazy or are you?" he angrily asked the scout.

"Both" was the reply and the scout relaxed, smiled, and leaned over the desk, reaching out to receive his money.

11   The horrified inspector cleared the window in one leap. He was seen in Washington, D.C., the following morning, having run full speed during the night. It was the last time Indian scouts were required to know English and applications for interpreter were being taken the following morning.

12   The problems of the missionaries in the early days provided stories which have become classics in Indian country. They are retold over and over again wherever Indians gather.

13   One story concerns a very obnoxious missionary who delighted in scaring the people with tales of hell, eternal fires, and everlasting damnation. This man was very unpopular and people went out of their way to avoid him. But he persisted to contrast heaven and hell as a carrot-and-stick technique of conversion.

14   One Sunday after a particularly fearful description of hell he asked an old chief, the main holdout of the tribe against Christianity, where he wanted to go. The old chief asked the missionary where *he* was going. And the missionary replied that, of course, he as a missionary of the gospel was going to heaven.

15   "Then I'll go to hell," the old chief said, intent on having peace in the world to come if not in this world.

16   On the Standing Rock reservation in South Dakota my grandfather served as the Episcopal missionary for years after his conversion to Christianity. He spent a great deal of his time trying to convert old Chief Gall, one of the strategists of Custer's demise, and a very famous and influential member of the tribe.

17   My grandfather gave Gall every argument in the book and some outside the book but the old man was adamant in keeping his old Indian ways. Neither the joys of heaven nor the perils of hell would sway the old man. But finally, because he was fond of my grandfather, he decided to become an Episcopalian.

18   He was baptized and by Christmas of that year was ready to take his first communion. He fasted all day and attended the Christmas Eve services that evening.

19   The weather was bitterly cold and the little church was heated by an old wood stove placed in the center of the church. Gall, as the most respected member of the community, was given the seat of honor next to the stove where he could keep warm.

20   In deference to the old man, my grandfather offered him communion first. Gall took the chalice and drained the entire supply of wine before returning to his seat. The wine had been intended for the entire congregation and so the old man had a substantial amount of spiritual refreshment.

21   Upon returning to his warm seat by the stove, it was not long before the wine took its toll on the old man who by now had had nothing to eat for nearly a day.

22   "Grandson," he called to my grandfather, "now I see why you wanted me to become a Christian. I feel fine, so nice and warm and happy. Why didn't you tell me that Christians did this every Sunday. If you had told me about this, I would have joined your church years ago."

23   Needless to say, the service was concluded as rapidly as possible and attendance skyrocketed the following Sunday.

24   Another missionary was traveling from Gallup to Albuquerque in the early days. Along the way he offered a ride to an Indian who was walking to town. Feeling he had a captive audience, he began cautiously to promote his message, using a soft-sell approach.

"Do you realize," he said, "that you are going to a place where sinners abound?"

The Indian nodded his head in assent.

"And the wicked dwell in the depths of their iniquities?"

Again a nod.

"And sinful women who have lived a bad life go?"

A smile and then another nod.

"And no one who lives a good life goes there?"

A possible conversion, thought the missionary, and so he pulled out his punch line: "And do you know what we call that place?"

25   The Indian turned, looked the missionary in the eye, and said, "Albuquerque." . . . .

26   One solution to the "Indian problem" advocated in the Eisenhower years was closing the rolls of Indians eligible to receive federal services. Instead of federal services, each Indian would receive a set per capita share of the total budget. As each Indian died off, the total budget would be reduced. When all of the eligible Indians died off, that would be the end of federal-Indian relationships.

27   This plan was the favorite solution of Commissioner Glenn Emmons, who was heading the bureau at that time. But try as he might, he couldn't sell the program to anyone.

28   An agency superintendent from the Rosebud Sioux reservation in South Dakota had to go to Washington on business and so he decided to drive. As

long as he was going he decided to take an old full blood with him to let the old man see the nation's capital.

29   The old man was very excited to be going to Washington and he made up his mind to see the Commissioner when he arrived there. So the superintendent began to suggest that the old man might have some solution to the Indian problem that he could share with the Commissioner. The old Indian discussed several ideas but admitted that they would probably be rejected.

30   Finally the superintendent outlined Emmon's plan to distribute the federal budget being spent on Indians among those then eligible for services. The old man pondered the idea for some time. Then he said, "That's the craziest idea I ever heard of. If I said something like that to the Commissioner, he would have me thrown out of his office."

31   Later the superintendent said he had always wished that the old man had suggested the plan to Emmons. "I always wanted," he told me, "to see the look on Emmon's face when an uneducated full blood suggested his own plan to him. I'd bet my last dollar that things would have changed at the BIA."

32   Frequently, without intending any humor, Indians can create a situation that is so funny that it is nearly impossible to believe. At the Manpower Conference in Kansas City in 1967 a series of events set up a hilarious incident. At least, looking back at it, Indians still chuckle over the results of the conference.

33   In 1966, after Philleo Nash had been Commissioner and had been fired for protecting the tribes, Udall gathered all of his top people and began to plan for a massive new program for "his" Indians. The administration also planned a comprehensive survey of Indian problems, perhaps realizing that Interior would once again draw a blank.

34   All of 1966 a secret Presidential Task Force surveyed Indian Affairs. By late December of that year they had compiled their report which, among other things, advocated a transfer of the Bureau of Indian Affairs from Interior to Health, Education and Welfare. Rumors began to fly in Indian country about the impending transfer and so the administration sent John Gardner, then Secretary of HEW, to Kansas City to present the idea to the assembled tribes.

35   In spite of all we could do to get HEW to advance the idea to a series of small conferences made up of influential tribal leaders, HEW insisted on presenting the idea to the entire group of assembled tribes—cold. So Gardner embarked for Kansas City with the usual entourage of high officialdom to present the message.

36   The tribal chairmen were greatly concerned about the possible loss of treaty rights which might occur during the transfer. When Gardner finished his presentation he opened the floor for questions, and the concerned chairmen began.

37   The first man wanted to know if all treaty rights would be protected. The Secretary of HEW assured him that treaty rights would be protected by law. The second man said that he had had such assurances before and now he wanted Gardner to give him his personal assurance so he could go back and talk with his people. Gardner gave him the personal assurances he wanted.

38   The next chairman wanted Gardner's assurance that nothing would be changed in the method of operations. The third wanted Gardner's assurance that no part of the existing structure would be changed, but that only the name plates would be different. The man following again wanted assurance that nothing would be changed, absolutely nothing. Wearily Gardner explained that *nothing* would be changed, everything would remain the same, all personnel would remain the same.

39   Eight straight chairmen questioned Gardner, asking for assurances that the basic structure would remain absolutely as it had been under Interior. Not a jot or tittle, according to Gardner, would be changed at all. There was no possible way that anything could be changed. Everything was to remain just as it was.

40   The ninth questioner brought down the house. "Why," he inquired, "if there are to be no changes at all, do you want to transfer the bureau to HEW? It would be the same as it is now," he concluded.

41   It suddenly occurred to everyone that the chairmen had successfully trapped Gardner in a neat box from which there was no escape. Suffice it to say, there was no transfer.

42   Not only the bureau, but other agencies, became the subject of Indian humor. When the War on Poverty was announced, Indians were justly skeptical about the extravagant promises of the bureaucrats. The private organizations in the Indian field, organized as the Council on Indian Affairs, sponsored a Capital Conference on Poverty in Washington in May of 1966 to ensure that Indian poverty would be highlighted just prior to the passage of the poverty program in Congress.

43   Tribes from all over the nation attended the conference to present papers on the poverty existing on their reservations. Two Indians from the plains area were asked about their feelings on the proposed program.

44   "Well," one said, "if they bring that War on Poverty to our reservation, they'll know they've been in a fight."

45   At the same conference, Alex Chasing Hawk, a nationally famous Indian leader from Cheyenne River and a classic storyteller, related the following tale about poverty.

46   It seemed that a white man was introduced to an old chief in New York City. Taking a liking to the old man, the white man invited him to dinner. The old chief hadn't eaten a good steak in a long time and eagerly accepted. He finished one steak in no time and still looked hungry. So the white man offered to buy him another steak.

47   As they were waiting for the steak, the white man said, "Chief, I sure wish I had your appetite."

48   "I don't doubt it, white man," the chief said. "You took my land, you took my mountains and streams, you took my salmon and my buffalo. You took everything I had except my appetite and now you want that. Aren't you ever going to be satisfied?"

49   At one conference on urban renewal, an Indian startled the audience when he endorsed the program. All day he had advocated using the poverty program to solve Indian problems on the reservation. Then, when the discussion got around to urban renewal, he abruptly supported the program.

50   He was asked why he wanted the program. It was, he was assured, perfectly natural for black and Mexican people to support urban renewal because so many of their people lived in the cities. But it didn't make sense to the conference participants what good an urban program would do for reservation Indians.

51   "I know," the Indian replied, "that a great many blacks and Mexicans want the program because so many of their people live in the cities and these cities must be rebuilt to give them a better life. But the program would also mean a better life for my people. You see, after the cities are rebuilt and everyone is settled there, we are going to fence them off and run our buffalo all over the country again." . . . .

52   In the old days, after the buffalo were gone, the Sioux were reduced to eating dogs to keep alive. They had no meat of any kind and rabbits on the reservation were rare. Other tribes keep up the ribbing by announcing that the chef has prepared a special treat for the Sioux present at the annual banquet through the special cooperation of the local dog pound.

53   In 1964, Billy Mills, a Sioux from Pine Ridge, South Dakota, won the ten thousand meter run at the Olympics in Tokyo. Justly proud of Billy, the Sioux went all out to inform other tribes of his achievement. One day we were bragging about Billy's feat to the Coeur d'Alenes of Idaho, who politely nodded their heads in agreement.

54   Finally the wife of the chairman, Leona Garry, announced that Mills' running ability did not really surprise the Coeur d'Alenes. "After all," she said, "up here in Idaho, Sioux have to run far, fast, and often if they mean to stay alive." That ended the discussion of Sioux athletic ability for the evening.

55   Clyde Warrior, during his time, was perhaps the single greatest wit in Indian country. One day he announced that the bureau was preparing a special training program for the other tribes. When quizzed about how it differed from other programs in existence, he noted that it had a restriction of only a half-hour lunch period. "Otherwise," Clyde said, "they would have to be retrained after lunch."

56 Providing information to inquisitive whites has also proved humorous on occasion. At a night club in Washington, D.C., a group of Indians from North Dakota were gathered, taking the edge off their trip before returning home. One man, a very shy and handsome Chippewa, caught the eye of one of the entertainers. She began to talk with him about Indian life.

57 Did Indians still live in tents, she inquired. He admitted shyly that he sometimes lived in a tent in the summer time because it was cooler than a house. Question after question came and was answered by the same polite responses. The girl took quite a fancy to the Chippewa and he got more and more embarrassed at the attention.

58 Finally she wanted to know if Indians still raided wagon trains. He said no, they had stopped doing that a long time ago. She was heartbroken at hearing the news. "I sure would like to be raided by you," she said, and brought down the house.

59 Louie Sitting Crow, an old timer from Crow Creek, South Dakota, used to go into town and watch the tourists who traveled along Highway 16 in South Dakota to get to the Black Hills. One day at a filling station a car from New York pulled up and began filling its tank for the long drive.

60 A girl came over to talk with Louie. She asked him a great many questions about the Sioux and Louie answered as best he could. Yes, the Sioux were fierce warriors. Yes, the Sioux had once owned all of the state. Yes, they still wished for the old days.

61 Finally the girl asked if the Indians still scalped people. Louie, weary of the questions, replied, "Lady, remember, when you cross that river and head west, you will be in the land of the fiercest Indians on earth and you will be very lucky to get to the Black Hills alive. And you ask me if they still scalp. Let me tell you, it's worse than that. Now they take the whole head."

62 As Louie recalled, the car turned around and headed east after the tank was full of gas.

63 Southwestern Indians can get off a good one when they are inspired. A couple of years ago I was riding a bus from Santa Fe to Albuquerque late at night. The bus was late in leaving Santa Fe and seemed like it was taking forever to get on its way.

64 Two old men from one of the pueblos between the two cities were aboard and were obviously feeling contented àfter their night in town. They filled the time we were waiting for the bus to depart telling stories and as the bus got under way they began to make comments on its snail's pace.

65 The bus driver was in no humor to withstand a running commentary on the speed of the bus that night and so he turned around and said, "If you don't like the speed we're making, why don't you get out and walk?"

66   "Oh, we couldn't do that," one of the men said. "They don't expect us home until the bus gets in."

67   An Indian in Montana was arrested for driving while intoxicated and he was thrown in jail for the night. The following morning he was hauled before the judge for his hearing. Not knowing English very well, the Indian worried about the hearing, but he was determined to do the best he could.

68   The judge, accustomed to articulate, English-speaking people appearing before him, waited for the man to make his plea. The Indian stood silently waiting for the judge to say something. As the two looked at each other the silence began to become unbearable and the judge completely forgot what the man was being tried for.

69   Finally he said, "Well, speak up, Indian, why are you here?"

70   The Indian, who had been planning to plead not guilty, was also completely off balance. He gulped, looked at the judge, and said, "Your honor, I was arrested for driving a drunken car."

71   One-line retorts are common in Indian country. Popovi Da, the great Pueblo artist, was quizzed one day on why the Indians were the first ones on this continent. "We had reservations," was his reply. Another time, when questioned by an anthropologist on what the Indians called America before the white man came, an Indian said simply, *"Ours."* A young Indian was asked one day at a conference what a peace treaty was. He replied, "That's when the white man wants a piece of your land."

72   The best example of Indian humor and militancy I have ever heard was given by Clyde Warrior one day. He was talking with a group of people about the National Indian Youth Council, of which he was then president, and its program for a revitalization of Indian life. Several in the crowd were skeptical about the idea of rebuilding Indian communities along traditional Indian lines.

73   "Do you realize," he said, "that when the United States was founded, it was only 5 percent urban and 95 percent rural and now it is 70 percent urban and 30 percent rural?"

74   His listeners nodded solemnly but didn't seem to understand what he was driving at.

75   "Don't you realize what this means?" he rapidly continued. "It means we are pushing them into the cities. Soon we will have the country back again."

76   Whether Indian jokes will eventually come to have more significance than that, I cannot speculate. Humor, all Indians will agree, is the cement by which the coming Indian movement is held together. When a people can laugh at themselves and laugh at others and hold all aspects of life together without letting anybody drive them to extremes, then it seems to me that that people can survive.

◆ Understanding Each Other: Discussion Questions

1. How important is humor to Native-Americans? How important is it in your culture? Do Indians laugh at themselves? When you make jokes in your culture, do you poke fun at yourselves?

2. What myths do people have about Native-Americans? What Hollywood stereotypes are there of Indians? What images of Indians did you have before you came to the United States?

3. According to Deloria, what was life like for Indians in the early days of the reservations? What tribes are mentioned?

4. An *allusion* is a rhetorical device which enriches the meaning of a passage by calling up a specific person, place, or event—real or imaginary. It can be a direct or an indirect reference. Writers of both fiction and nonfiction use this device. Deloria makes several allusions in this excerpt. Use an encyclopedia and an English-English dictionary to identify the following: the Minnesota Wars; the Standing Rock Reservation; Chief Gall; Custer's demise; Gallup; Albuquerque; the Eisenhower years; Commissioner Glenn Emmons; the Rosebud Sioux Reservation; Udall; the Department of the Interior; John Gardner; the War on Poverty; the Council On Indian Affairs; Alex Chasing Hawk; Billy Mills; the Black Hills; Popovi Da; Clyde Warrior.

5. What do these idioms mean? If you can, ask a native speaker.

collective psyche	a full blood
carrot-and-stick technique	jot or tittle
soft-sell approach	urban renewal
punch line	go at a snail's pace
look someone in the eye	one-line retort

6. What do the abbreviations BIA and HEW stand for?

7. Some anthropologists believe that Native-Americans migrated from Asia across a land link to the North American Continent. Research this subject in a library. Is there any definite linguistic or cultural proof of this migration? What do you think?

8. When were "the old days" that Deloria talks about in paragraph 52?

9. What is the point of the joke Alex Chasing Hawk told about the white man who invites an old Indian chief to dinner in New York City?

10. The buffalo was *very* important to the Plains Indians: it provided food, bones for knives and tools, hide for clothes and shoes and tepees, skins for blankets and robes, fat for cooking, and dung for fires. In view of this, explain the joke in the story about the Indian who endorses an urban-renewal program.

♦ Interactive Grammar and Usage: Rules in Reflection

Correct noun and pronoun reference is critical to clarity in English. For practice in this area, work with a peer to fill in the blanks below. Your teacher may give you a list of choices. Be prepared to explain your choices. Afterwards, generalize the usage rules implicit here. The first sentence is done for you.

At one conference on urban renewal, an Indian startled the audience when he endorsed the program. All day _____ had advocated using the poverty program to solve _____ problems on _____ reservation. Then, when the discussion got around to urban renewal, _____ abruptly supported _____ . _____ was asked why _____ wanted the program.

_____ was, _____ was assured, perfectly natural for
₈   ₉

black and Mexican people to support _____ because so many
                                                    ₁₀

of their people lived in _____ . But _____ didn't make
                                    ₁₁   ₁₂

sense to _____ what good an urban program would do for
                ₁₃

_____ .
        ₁₄

     " _____ know," the Indian replied, "that a great many
              ₁₅

_____ want _____ because so many of _____ live
        ₁₆   ₁₇   ₁₈

in the cities and these _____ must be rebuilt to give _____
                                ₁₉   ₂₀

a better life. But _____ would also mean _____ for my
                          ₂₁   ₂₂

people. _____ see, after _____ are rebuilt and
                ₂₃   ₂₄

_____ is settled there, _____ are going to fence
        ₂₅   ₂₆

_____ off and run our buffalo all over _____ again."
        ₂₇   ₂₈

♦ Increasing Word Power: Vocabulary in Context

Working with a partner, decide on the meaning *in context* of each of the following words or phrases. Then look up each item in a good English-English dictionary. Does the context meaning of the word in the reading differ in any way from the dictionary's definition? If so, how did the context help you understand the meaning of the word as used in the passage?

Word	Meaning in This Context	Dictionary Definition
irony		
satire		
granite-faced		
grunting		
perpetuated		
mythology		
scouts		
bureaucracies		
en route		
disband		
mustering-out		
wearily		
delirious		
obnoxious		

Word	Meaning in This Context	Dictionary Definition
damnation		
persisted		
adamant		
fond		
chalice		
skyrocketed		
assent		
per capita		
pondered		
hilarious		
chuckle		
be fired		
rumors		
be skeptical		
salmon		
startle		
get around to		
ribbing		
bragging		
raid		
scalp		
pueblos		
gulp		
revitalization		
speculate		
cement		

♦ Finding Your Own Voice: For Discussion and Writing

1. Go to the U.S. Documents section of your library and research the treaties between Native-Americans and the government of the United States. What do those treaties promise? How many of those treaties were broken? How many of them are still in effect today?
2. Americans often protest injustices by writing letters to the editors of newspapers or magazines. Find a letter of protest in a newspaper and use it as a model to write your own letter protesting an unfair practice.
3. Conditions on some Indian reservations are very bad, and educational opportunities for some Native-American children are very poor. What can and should be done about this? Write an article or a letter to an important newspaper like the *New York Times,* the *Washington Post,* or the *Christian Science Monitor,* suggesting what ought to be done.

4. Write an anecdote about something funny that has happened to you since you arrived in the United States. Share it with your classmates.
5. Perform the scenario "Food for thought" to bring your work with this chapter full circle. Your teacher may ask you to write an essay about the theme of this scenario, by yourself or with a team of other students.

CHAPTER 10

Russian American

♦ Listening to Each Other: Scenario

See Chapter 1 for instructions on how to perform a scenario.
Prepare and perform the scenario "Look who's coming to dinner!"

♦ Speaking Out: Debriefing Questions

1. Who had solutions to the dilemma posed in the scenario? Are any other solutions possible?
2. How was the dilemma in the scenario resolved?
3. Did you identify with anyone in the scenario? Why did you empathize with that person?
4. If the scenario were acted out again, would you do or say anything different?
5. Have you ever faced the same dilemma as the one in the scenario? Did it involve family members? How did you resolve your dilemma?

♦ Reaching Out: Suggestions for Further Activities

1. Write a scenario about how young women and young men in your country arrange to meet during courting. Have the class act out the scene.
2. Bring in a table setting—dishes, eating utensils, glasses, cups, bowls, flower arrangements, napkins, tablecloths, and any other items used in

your home—and demonstrate correct table etiquette of your native country.

3. If possible, watch the film *Moscow-on-the-Hudson*, starring Robin Williams. Take notes on the characters and on the story line. What are the central characters like? After reading the following excerpt from the book, compare the characterization and action of the movie and book versions.

4. Write an essay about one aspect of the scenario and bring it into class for the group to critique and polish.

♦ Reading: From *Moscow-on-the-Hudson*, by M. K. Argus

Read the following selection, keeping in mind the scenario you have already experienced. It is always a good idea to have an English-English dictionary at hand when you read. A useful technique is to read the selection through quickly the first time, highlighting words or phrases that you think you need to look up. Then go back and do a more careful reading, looking up unfamiliar words.

OH, TO BE MARRIED TO AN AMERICAN!

1   I owe my Americanization exclusively to the patience and perseverance of my wife. I am now able to spend an evening in the company of native Americans without committing more than the average husbandly quota of *faux pas*. Only by my accent, which not even my wife has been able to Americanize, can I be distinguished from other Americans.

2   It was not like this in the beginning, during the first few years of my married life. Now I can see clearly what was wrong with me, and I am able to appreciate fully the tremendous improvement in my habits, behavior, and table manners. The fact that occasionally, in a mood of rebellion or of self-pity, I begin to doubt whether I am better as an American than I was as a Russian is beside the point.

3   There is a story about a Russian and an American who were having dinner together in a restaurant. A stranger stopped at their table. The American looked up and said, "Oh, hello, John."

"Hello, Sam," answered the stranger.

"When did you arrive?"

"This morning."

"Staying long?"

"Two or three days."

"Ring me up tomorrow, and we'll have lunch together."

"All right, I will."

"So long. Be good."

"So long."

4   The stranger left. "That was my brother John," said the American. "Haven't seen each other in six years."

5   Another man approached the table. The Russian jumped up, ran over to the newcomer, shook his hand violently, embraced him, grabbed him by the arm and dragged him over to the table.

6   "Sam," said the Russian to the American, "I want you to meet my dearest friend, a splendid fellow, Ivan Ivanovich. I met him last night at a party."

7   I was like the Russian in the story. Now I am different. I used to be expansive, excitable, volatile, talkative, amicable, and frank. No more. I am now an American.

8   It took me a long time to discover that half of the questions Americans ask you need not be answered because no reply is expected. In the days when I was still green and naïve I even used to consider a simple "how do you do" as a sort of interrogation. It flattered me to know that a person whom I hardly knew was interested enough in my welfare to inquire courteously how did I do. I would answer the query at great length and give a detailed account of the state of my health and finances. But then someone explained to me that "how do you do" was not a question but a positive statement calling in return for a no less positive "how do you do."

9   I also did not realize that Americans who inquired about one's health were not at all interested in it. It was my wife who taught me to answer "fine, thank you" to any such inquiry, even if I were on the verge of a nervous collapse or about to undergo a most serious operation.

10   Russians are different. When I ask another Russian how he feels, I expect an answer. I would be offended if he did not tell me what was wrong with him. That "fine, thank you" business is sufficient for Americans but not for us. Anyway, no self-respecting Russian, even in the pink of condition, would be satisfied with so meaningless an answer. We too are entitled to some fun.

11   Americans, of course, are extremely courteous. Russians are not. They click their heels, kiss ladies' hands, but otherwise are rude, uncouth, and tactless.

12   Suppose you want to ask an American for a favor. You call him up on the telephone and make an appointment. You come to see him on the specified hour. The American listens politely to what you have to tell him. He never interrupts you except for occasional exclamations such as "you don't say!" "really?" or "gosh!" When you are finished with your story, he offers you a cigarette, maybe a cigar. He may even invite you to lunch. Naturally he will not do anything for you; he never intended to. But he does nothing for you in so charming, courteous, and pleasant a way that you are eternally grateful to him and always refer to him as an "awfully nice person."

13   Not so a Russian. If you want a Russian to do something for you, you call him up on the telephone and make an appointment. You come to see him on the specified hour, but he is not there. Either he was there an hour before you came, or he will appear two hours later. You finally succeed in get-

ting hold of him. You corner him and make a desperate attempt to tell him the nature of your request. He keeps interrupting you. You get angry. A heated argument ensues. You call each other uncomplimentary names. Then you both subside, ask each other's forgiveness, and go out to celebrate the re-establishment of pacific relations. After a couple of drinks the Russian presses you to his bosom, tells you that you are his best and dearest friend, and promises to do everything in the world for you. The Russian will actually do something for you, but, having expected so much of him, you will always remain unrequited and consider him a most unpleasant character.

14   I am no longer an unpleasant character. I am thoroughly Americanized, and my wife takes great pride in the knowledge that other people consider me a very nice and courteous person.

15   One Russian trait was not easily eradicated. My Americanization must have hit a subconscious snag at that particular point and left a blank spot. Whenever American friends or acquaintances tell us, "So glad to have seen you, we must get together again real soon," I immediately jump at the suggestion and cry impulsively, "Of course, of course, it will be a pleasure. How about next Friday? We are not doing anything next Friday."

16   Scores of times but, I fear, still rather unsuccessfully, my wife has tried to impress on my credulous Continental mind the maxim that when an American says, "We must get together real soon," he has no particular desire to see me for at least six months.

17   Russians are built differently. When a Russian tells you that "we ought to get together real soon" he means *soon*, even tomorrow. If a Russian does not want to see you he does not invite you, but if he does invite you, he sincerely means it although he may not be at home when you call on him. This is an old Russian tradition. The Russian will ask you to visit him on a certain date. He will insist that you bring some friends along. He will urge you to come early "so we can have a long conversation." Then he will forget all about it and, in his turn, accept some other Russian's invitation. If you are a true Russian, you will forget to come on the appointed day or, at least, be a day or two late. This, according to our code of behavior, is never held against you.

18   Once I spent a long evening with a Russian friend discussing Pushkin and the ills of the world.

"It was a very pleasant evening," my friend said (a pleasant evening to a Russian is one in which he manages to talk twice as much as his companion).

"Oh, yes," I agreed. "We must get together again very soon. How about next week?"

"Next week?" my friend contemptuously brushed aside the suggestion. "Why wait until next week? Let us meet again tomorrow. No, why wait until tomorrow? Tonight! Yes, tonight. Let us go to my house. My wife will be glad to see you. She will serve us some tea, and we will have a nice discussion."

"Isn't it a bit too late?" I queried my friend.

"Bah," he said. "It is never too late. Remember our proverb, 'better late than never.'"

19   I cannot truthfully say that my friend's wife was overly enthusiastic about our decision, but she served us some tea, and we had a wonderful discussion about Pushkin and the ills of the world.

20   As a true Russian I should have invited my friend and his wife right there and then to *my* house. But I remembered my American wife and her incomprehensible ways. She would not have understood such a generous Russian gesture: when I invite a Russian friend to my house, I must warn my wife twenty-four hours in advance and cancel the invitation twelve hours later.

21   The Americanization of manners, especially table manners, was also a painful and tedious process which required a vast amount of tact and ingenuity on the part of my wife.

22   I still kiss ladies' hands but only because American ladies expect Russian gentlemen to do it. I personally detest kissing ladies' hands. I never practiced this worldly art in Russia and only learned it in this country.

23   My table manners are a source of constant anguish to my wife and me. Russians like to eat. But the food, once it is served, becomes less important than the general dining-room atmosphere. We like to get through with the meal as quickly as possible and then linger around the table. When a plate is served, a Russian grabs a fork with his left hand and a knife with his right, lowers his eyes, and begins to swallow the contents of his plate. In a few minutes he is through. The Americans have not yet begun to eat; they are still busy with the preliminary chewing of celery—the vegetable that even Americanized Russians (such as I am) view with suspicion and distrust. When the Russian discovers that he is the only one at the table with a surplus of time, he delivers a monologue on some important current topic.

24   It was after I had delivered such a monologue that my wife gave me the first lesson in American table manners.

"You know," she said after the guests had gone, "you scared the wits out of poor Mrs. Fisher. Must you discuss politics with your knife and fork?"

"No," I answered, "I can discuss politics with my bare hands."

"It isn't nice," my wife continued. "Russians perhaps don't mind it [this has become her standard expression when explaining the intricacies of American manners: "Russians perhaps don't mind it"]. But it is not nice for one person to monopolize the conversation, and more so since you are the host. You should let your guests say something, too. Everyone, you know, is entitled to his opinion. If a guest of yours makes a statement which you don't like or with which you don't agree, just smile pleasantly but do not start an argument with him."

"I will try," I promised, thinking sadly that in Russia I would have thrown such a guest out of my house.

"And by the way," continued my wife, "why don't you chew your food? It is much better for your digestion, and it looks better, too. A host should never finish eating before his guests. It makes them uncomfortable; they get the feeling that they are eating an awful lot."

25 I promised to chew my food.

26 "One more thing," my wife said. "You don't have to eat with both hands. It may be all right in Russia, but here it is considered poor manners. Do try to keep your left hand under the table. It is so much easier."

27 I promised to keep my left hand under the table, but I still do not understand what gave Americans the idea that it was easier to eat with one hand concealed than with both hands.

28 There was also trouble with my tea drinking. I always drink tea in a glass. Even now, with an American wife and American citizenship papers, I must have my tea in a glass. Can anyone imagine an Alabaman or Tennessean ordering a Coca-Cola in a cup? It cannot be done; it is preposterous. Tea, like Coca-Cola, does not taste right in a cup.

29 My wife conceded the point, but I too had to make a concession—the spoon. The spoon plays a major part in Russian tea drinking. It is not only a device for stirring the sugar. It is also an important instrument that enables one to balance the hot glass steadily in one's hand. The spoon, after it has served its stirring purpose, remains in the glass while the drinker's forefinger rests on its handle, and the glass itself fits snugly into his palm. It is really very simple and convenient.

30 The question of the spoon came up shortly after our marriage when my wife was still trying to approach me with a certain measure of tact. We had spent an evening at a friend's (her friend's) house. On the way home she said, "About the spoon, dear."

"Which spoon?"

"The teaspoon. You keep it in your glass while you drink your tea. Doesn't it bother you?"

"No, why should it bother me?"

"You must be terribly uncomfortable. It can get into your eye or break your spectacles."

"Don't be afraid," I reassured my wife. "No danger of that. I never heard of anyone hurting his eye while drinking tea."

"Everyone was looking at you," said my wife.

"At me? Why?"

"At the way you drank your tea. With the spoon in the glass, I mean. I was quite embarrassed."

"Why should you have been embarrassed?"

"On account of you. We don't drink tea like that. I cannot go around explaining to everyone that this is the Russian way of drinking tea. Can't you try to drink your tea without the spoon in your glass? Just for my sake, dear. Next time try to remember to leave the spoon on the saucer."

31   And so, no spoon in my tea glass No more fork-and-knife discussions at the dinner table. No more arguments with anyone claiming the diplomatic immunity of a guest. No more rash promises to Russians who come to me for advice. I eat celery before dinner. I chew my food. I cut up my meat into small unappetizing morsels, place the knife on the edge of the plate, hide my left hand under the table, grasp the fork with my right hand, and make the best of a tortuous meal. No more do I pick up the olives with a spoon, as we used to do in the old country; I use my fingers to the horror and consternation of my compatriots. When a Russian comes to me for a favor, I listen to him attentively and never interrupt him except for occasional exclamations in the Russian equivalent of "gosh!" "really?" "you don't say!" Then I invite him to lunch and assure him that he is a magnificent fellow deserving of better luck. When during a heated political discussion in my house one of my guests makes some silly statement, I jovially slap the idiot on his shoulder and exclaim with true American open-mindedness, "Well, old boy, there is something to what you are saying."

32   Oh, yes, I am an American.

33   But whenever I dine in a Russian home, someone invariably points to the left arm that my American wife taught me to hide under the table and inquires with genuine concern, "Did you hurt it? Or is it arthritis?"

from *Moscow-on-the-Hudson* by M. K. Argus. Copyright 1948, 1949, 1951 by Mikhail Eisenstadt Jeleznov. Reprinted by permission of Harper Collins Publishers, Inc.

♦ Understanding Each Other: Discussion Questions

1. Are you or is anyone you know married to an American? What kinds of adjustments did both partners have to make?

2. What does the phrase *faux pas* mean? What kinds of actions are considered to be *faux pas* in your culture? What kinds of table manners are customary in your culture?

3. Explain the meaning of the following phrases: to owe something to someone; to be green and naïve; to be flattered by; to be on the verge of; a nervous collapse; to be offended; in the pink of condition; to be entitled to; to corner; the nature of something; to remain unrequited; to hit a snag; to be built differently; the ills of the world; the appointed day; to manage to do; to brush aside; to scare the wits out of someone; to monopolize the conversation; to concede something; to make a concession; to fit snugly; a certain measure; for someone's sake; diplomatic immunity; to slap on the shoulder.

4. What differences between Russian habits and American habits does Argus describe in this chapter?

5. Do you or does someone you know behave in any way like the narrator? Do you believe that human nature is fairly similar regardless of national background? Do cultural habits and traditions sometimes *force* us to be different?

6. Who was Aleksandr Pushkin? When did he live? Find a biographical entry on him in an encyclopedia. Why is he important in Russian culture?

7. If you are invited to a Russian's house, what are you supposed to do if you are a "true Russian," according to Argus? Would this behavior be considered acceptable in your culture?

8. What does "code of behavior" mean? What "codes" do Americans follow? What "codes" do the people in your native land follow?

9. What does the proverb "better late than never" mean? Do you have a proverb like it in your culture? How common do you think it is among languages?

10. What troubles does Argus have as he moves back and forth between American and Russian cultural traditions? What kinds of problems have you encountered in moving back and forth between cultures?

11. What habits did Argus's wife want him to change? What reasons does she give for wanting him to change?

◆ Interactive Grammar and Usage: Rules in Reflection

Coherency in English writing can be promoted by using verb tenses and parallel word forms consistently and by repeating key words or phrases. For practice in these areas, work with a partner and fill in the blanks below. Your teacher may give you a list of choices. Be ready to explain the reasons for each answer and the grammar rules implicit here. Some sentences have been partially completed for you, as examples.

Another man approached the table. The Russian <u>jumped up, ran over</u> to the newcomer, <u>shook</u> his hand violently, _____ him, __1__

_____ him by the arm and _____ him over to the __2__ __3__

table. . . .

I was like the Russian in the story. Now I am different. I used to be <u>ex-</u> <u>pansive</u>, _____ , _____ , _____ , __4__ __5__ __6__

_____ , and _____ . No more. I am _____ an __7__ __8__ __9__

American. . . .

Americans, of course, are extremely courteous. Russians _____ __10__

not. They <u>click their heels</u>, _____ ladies' hands, _____ __11__ __12__

are _____, uncouth, and _____. . . . __13__ __14__

I still _____ hands but only because American ladies expect __15__

Russian gentlemen to do it. _____ personally _____ kiss- __16__ __17__

<u>ing ladies' hands.</u> _____ _____ practiced this worldly art __18__ __19__

in _____ and _____ _____ it in _____ __20__ __21__ __22__ __23__

. . . .

My wife conceded the point, but I too had to make a concession—<u>the</u> <u>spoon.</u> _____ plays a major part in Russian tea drinking. __24__

_____ is _____ a device for stirring the sugar. __25__ __26__

_____ is _____ an important instrument that enables one __27__ __28__

to balance the hot glass steadily in one's hand. _____ , after __29__

_____ has served its stirring purpose, remains in the glass while __30__

the drinker's forefinger rests on _____ handle, and the glass itself __31__

fits snugly into his palm. It is really very simple and _____ . __32__

◆ Increasing Word Power: Vocabulary in Context

Working with a partner, decide on the meaning *in context* of each of the following words or phrases. Then look up each item in a good English-English dictionary. Does the context meaning of the word in the reading differ in any way from the dictionary's definition? If so, how did the context help you understand the meaning of the word as used in the passage?

Word	Meaning in This Context	Dictionary Definition
Americanization		
exclusively		
perseverance		
quota		
rebellion		
embraced		
splendid		
volatile		
amicable		
frank		
interrogation		
welfare		
query		
uncouth		
occasional		
exclamations		
ensue		
subside		
pacific		
bosom		
eradicated		
subconscious		
tedious		
ingenuity		
detest		
linger		
chew		
monologue		
intricacies		
digestion		
preposterous		
spectacles		
grasp		
tortuous		
consternation		

Word	Meaning in This Context	Dictionary Definition
compatriots		
jovially		
idiot		
invariably		
arthritis		

◆ Finding Your Own Voice: For Discussion and Writing

1. Have differences between your cultural habits or customs and those practiced in the United States caused you to have any unusual or embarrassing experiences since your arrival here? If so, share one of those experiences with the class—or tell them about something that happened to a friend.

2. With your classmates, write a play about people from different cultures who are trying to get to know each other despite the cultural barriers. The play can be funny, or sad, or both. Then cast and produce your play for other students in your school or for groups in the community. If possible, videotape it to show to others. Your play should take ten to fifteen minutes to perform.

3. Write an essay or story which illustrates good table manners and etiquette in your country. You might present it as a "guide" for travelers to your homeland.

4. Perform the scenario "A rain check or a strong aspirin" to bring your work with this chapter full circle. Your teacher may ask you to write an essay about the theme of this scenario, by yourself or with other students.